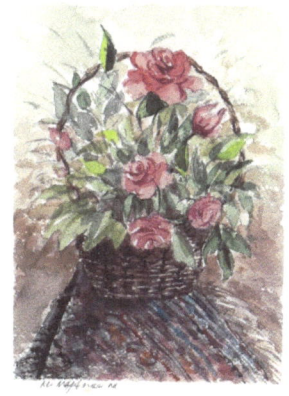 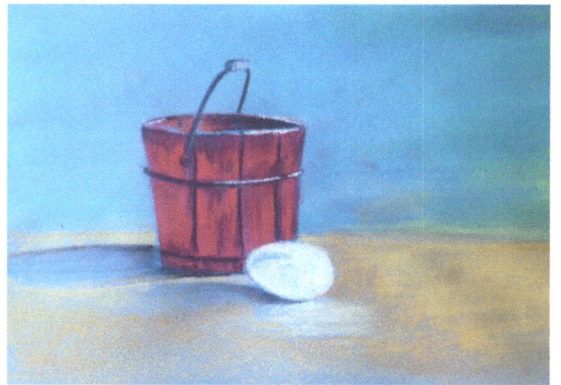 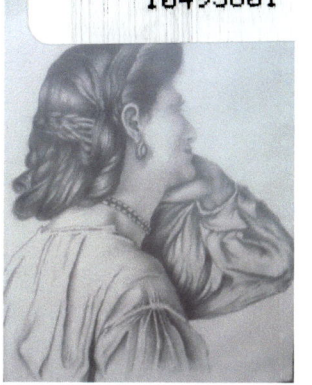

ART BOOK SERIES :

BOOK 3 -PASTEL WORKS

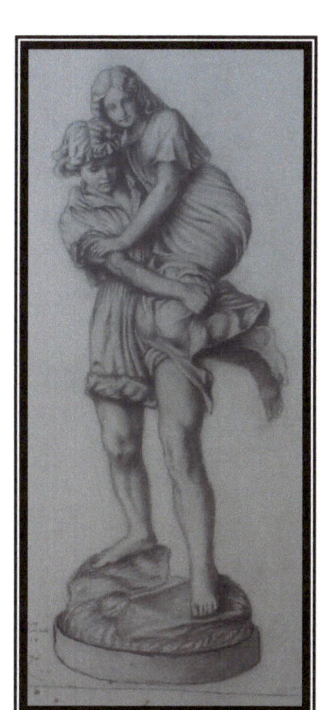 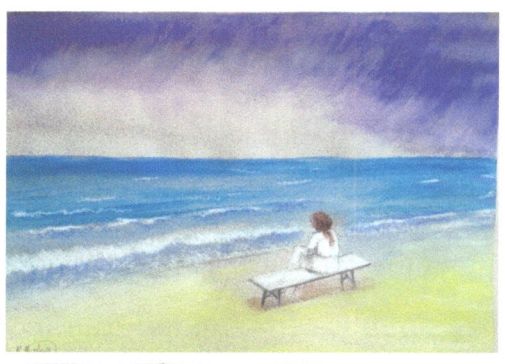 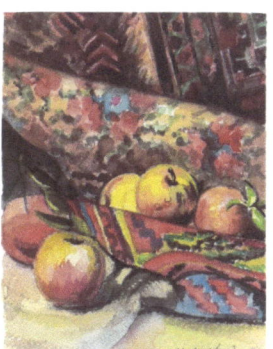

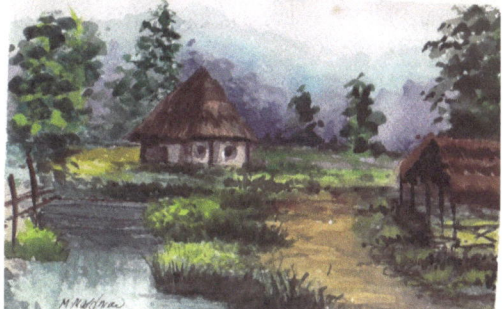 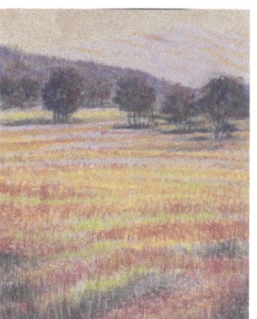

BY : MAJID MAJDNIA

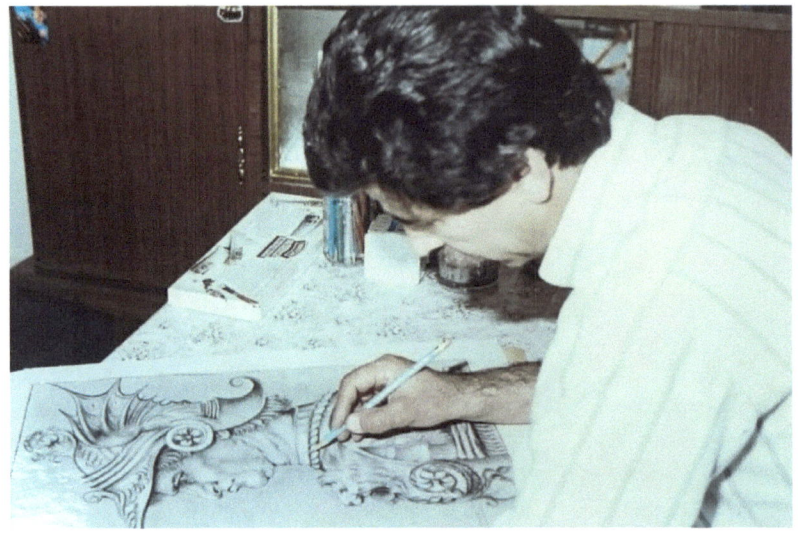

About the artist

Majid was born in 1952 in a crowded family. He showed an interest in drawing from early years of childhood. In cold winter days of the city, he carved his tiny sketches of birds, trees and flowers on icy windows. He spent hours watching art works in art shops and galleries. Majid studied linguistic and Italian language and later continued in communication to obtain his PHD degree. He had chances to directly establish and manage some publications as public relation and training manager of a financial organization, where he produced some art works. He used free times for drawing and painting . He always remained faithful to his main hobby.

He has published his pencil works and watercolor painting is book Nos 1 and 2. Now he is ready to publish his pastel works on sceneries.

Copy Rights @2019

All rights reserved.

ISBN: 9781070270623

Majdnia, Majid

INTRODUCTION

After publishing the watercolor painting works in Book-No.1 and pencil works on portrait in Book No.2 I am please and excited to share my pastel works on sceneries with Boon No.3.

I have included all works that I have produced while training and practice. Some of works are copies of famous works that taken from various books or magazines. It is not intended to own any of the original drawing.

The key points in color painting either pastel or oil painting and or watercolor is the study and knowledge of colors and their mixes. New learners and students are encouraged to practice with combinations of colors to master.

Majid Majdnia

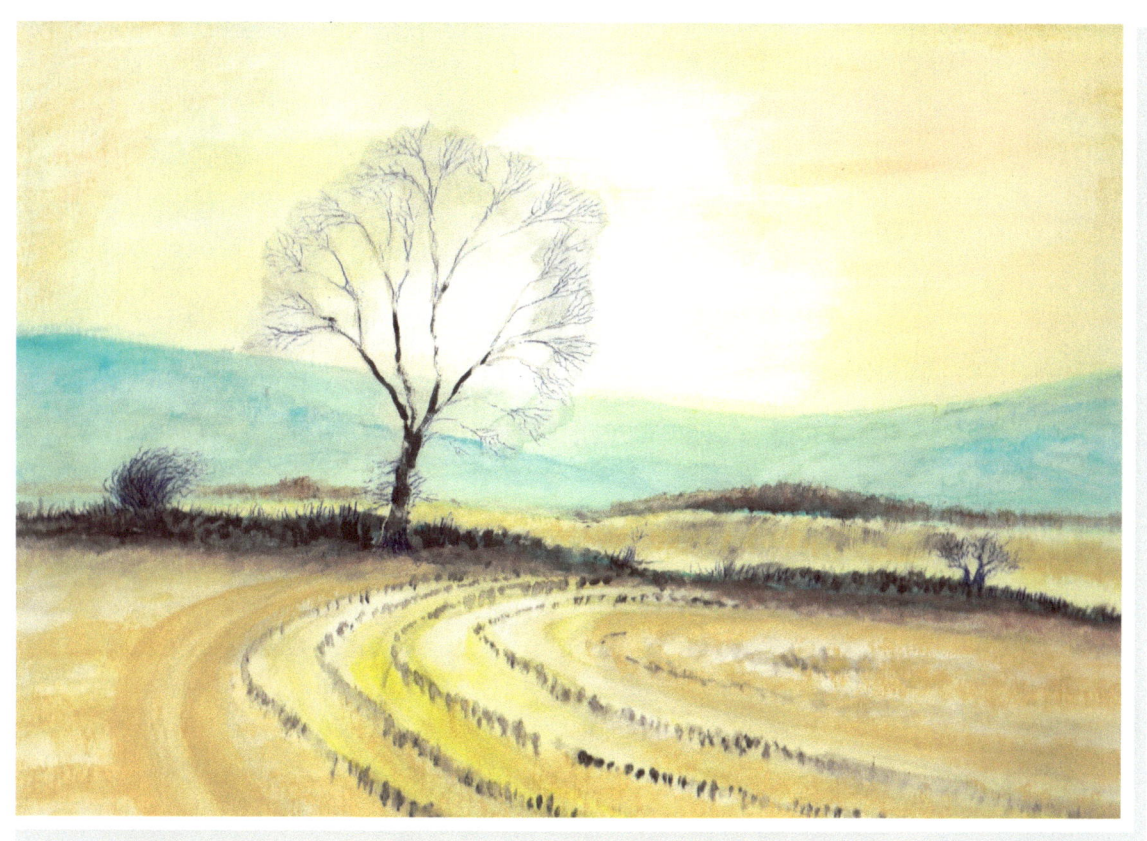

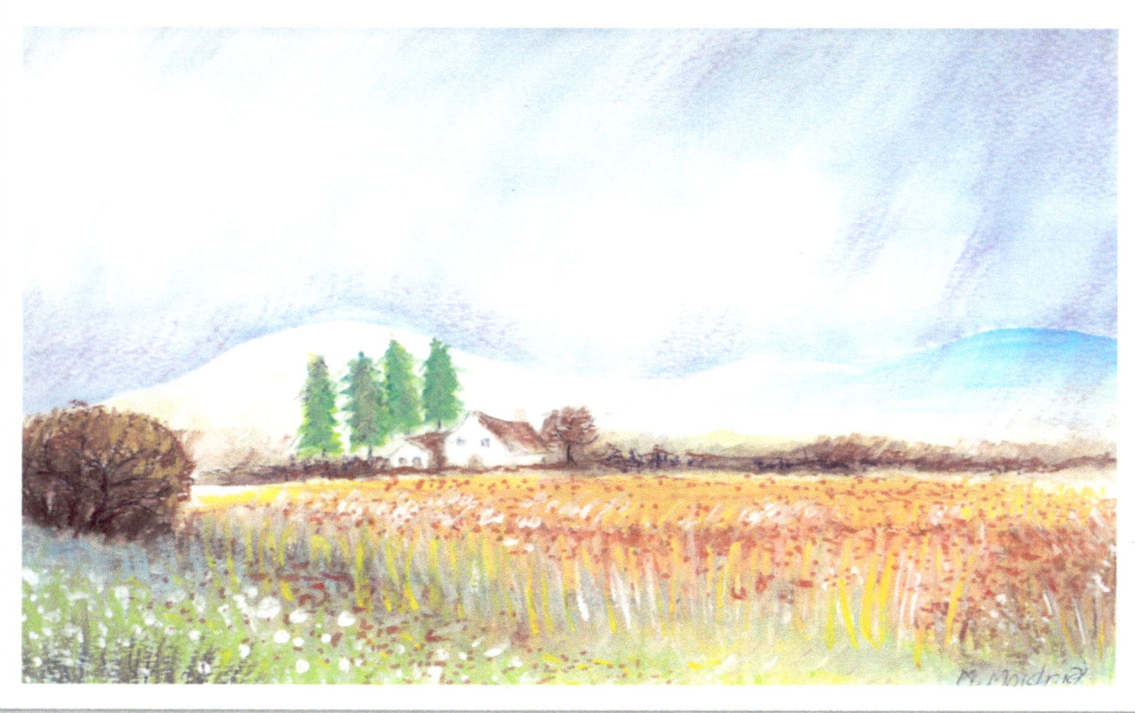

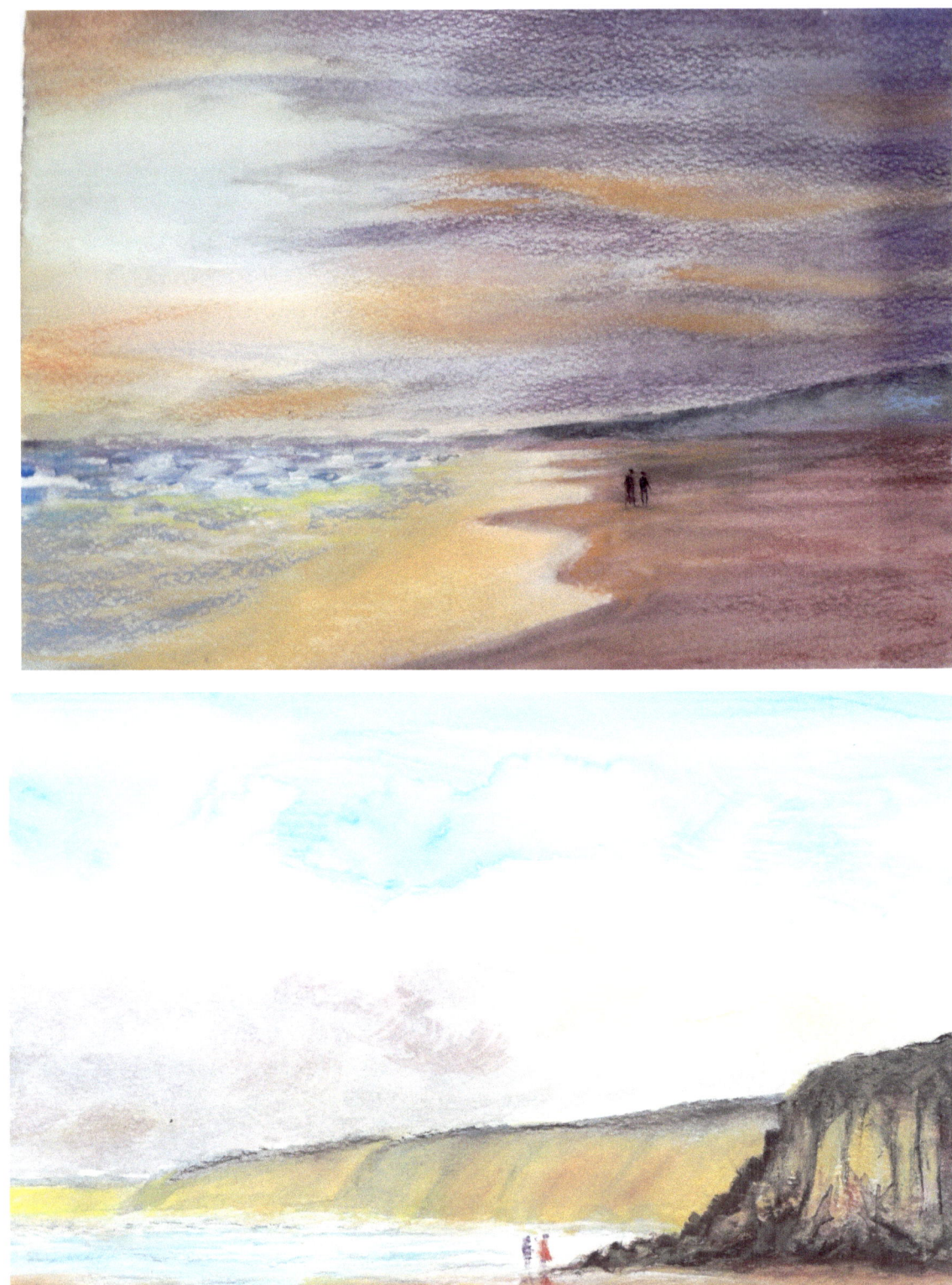

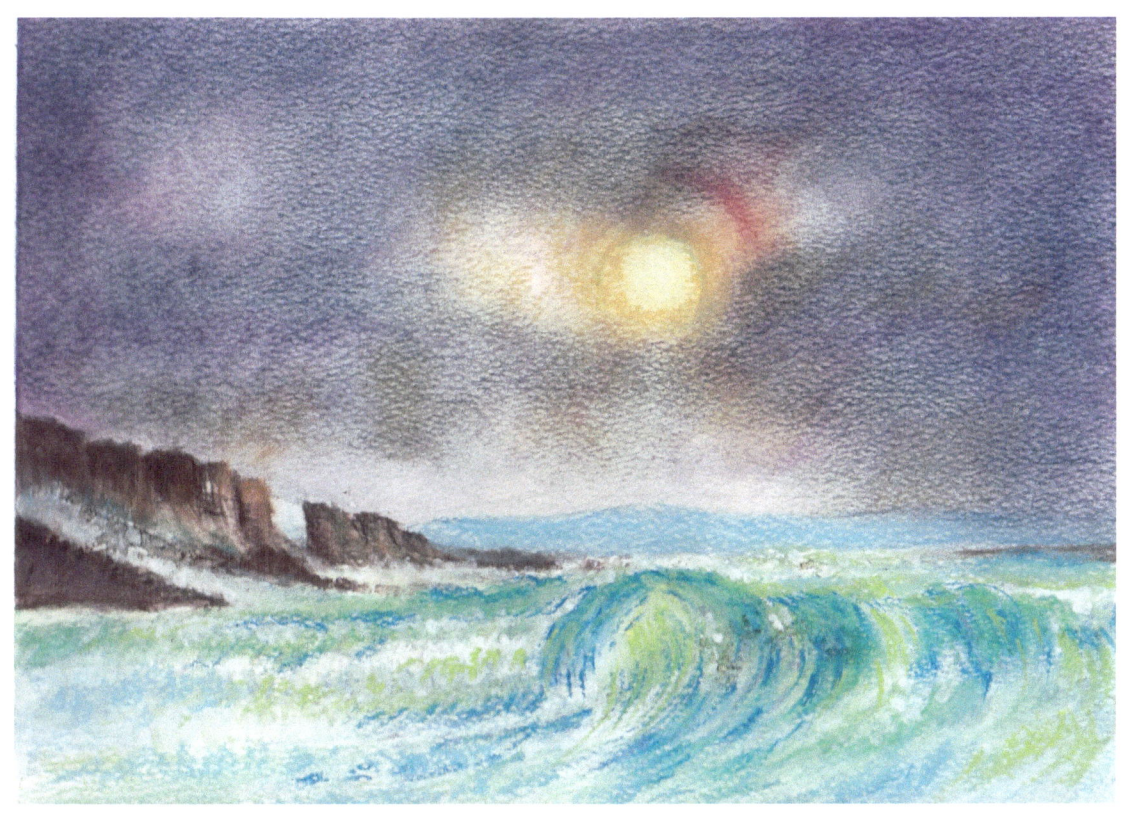

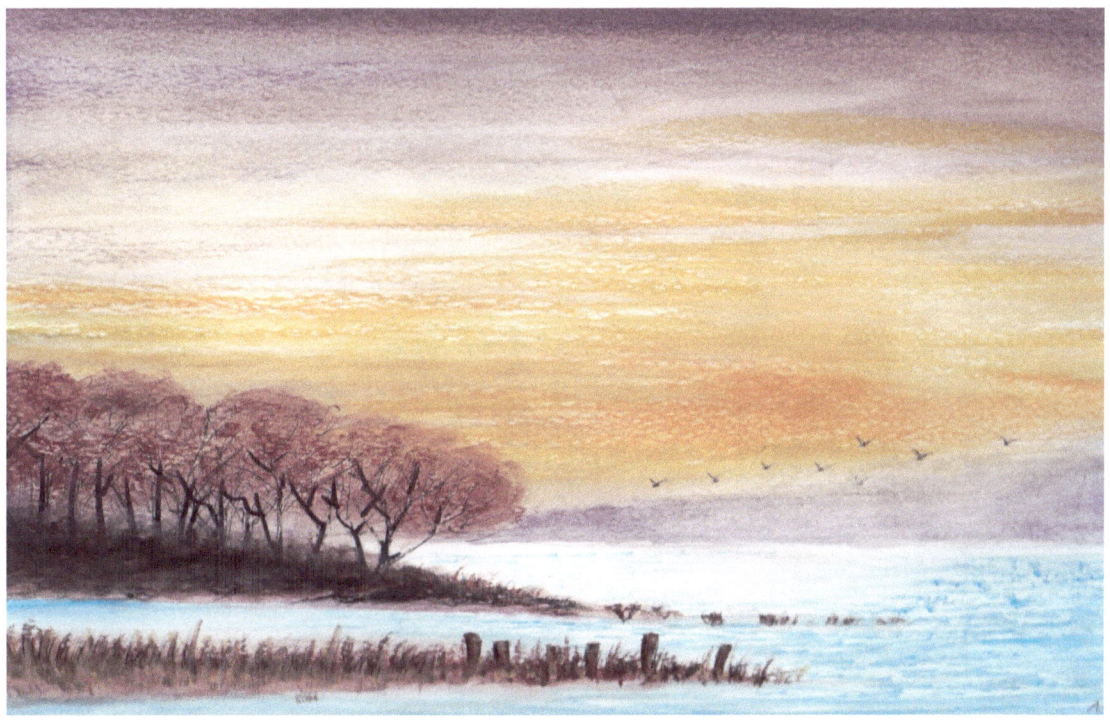

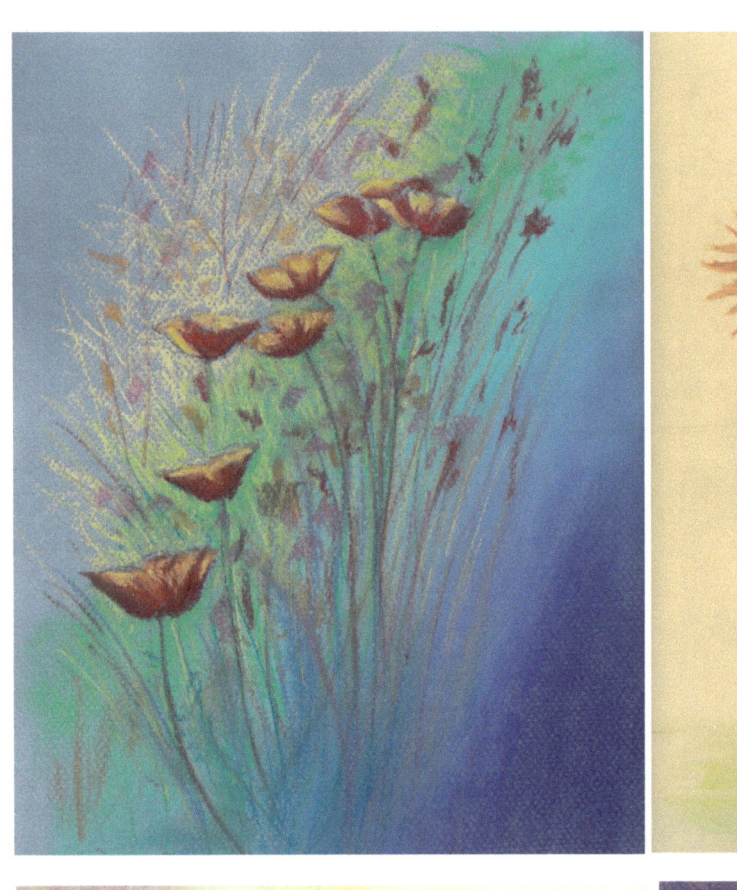
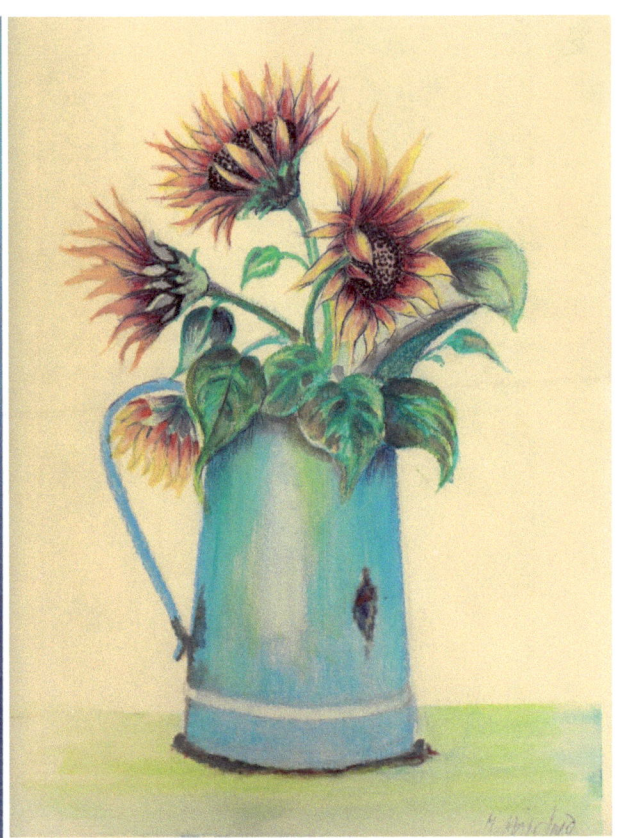
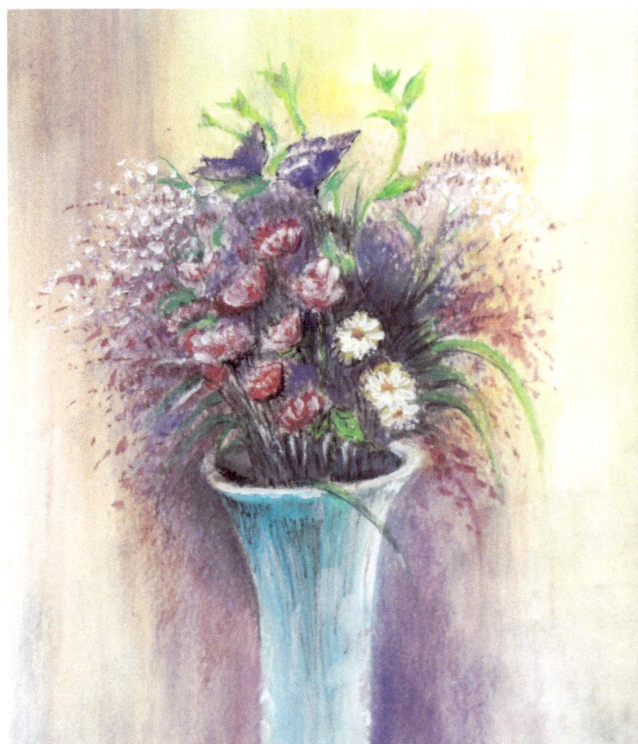
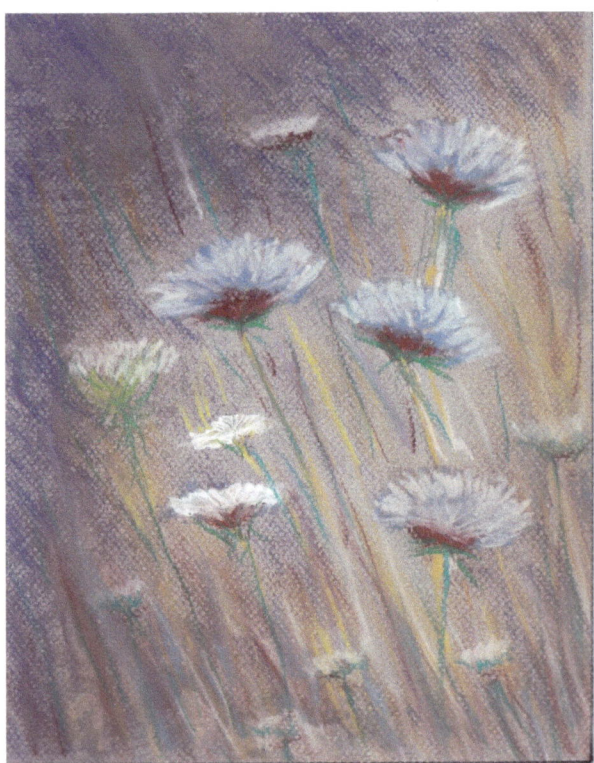

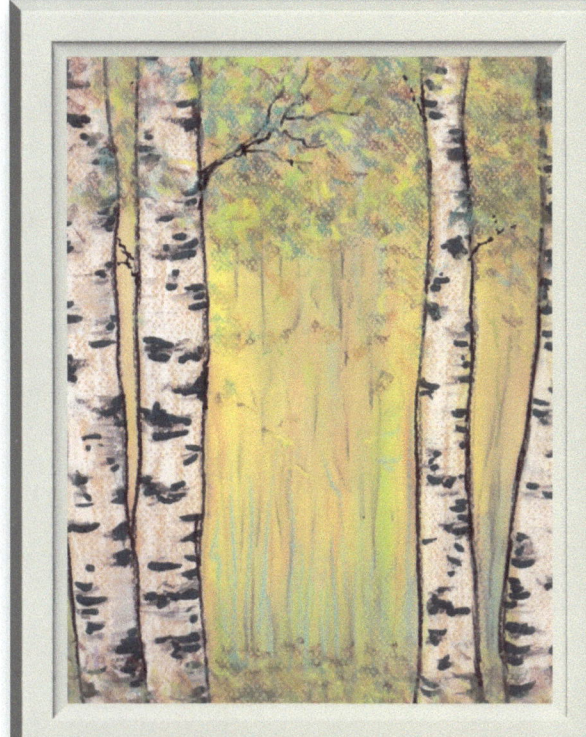
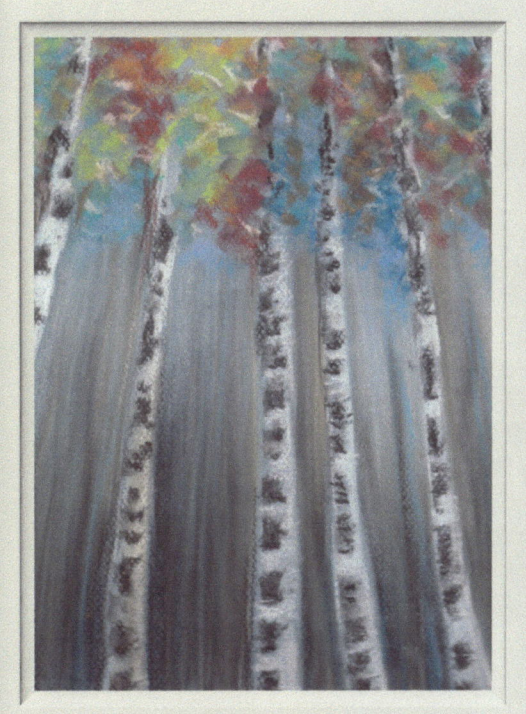
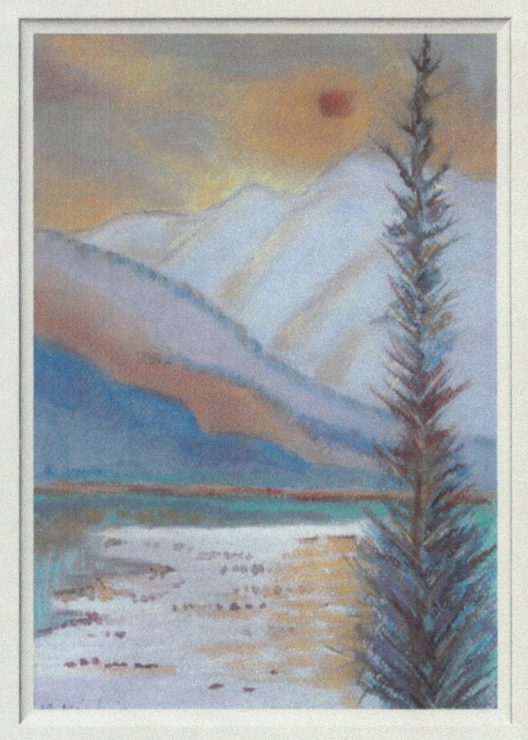
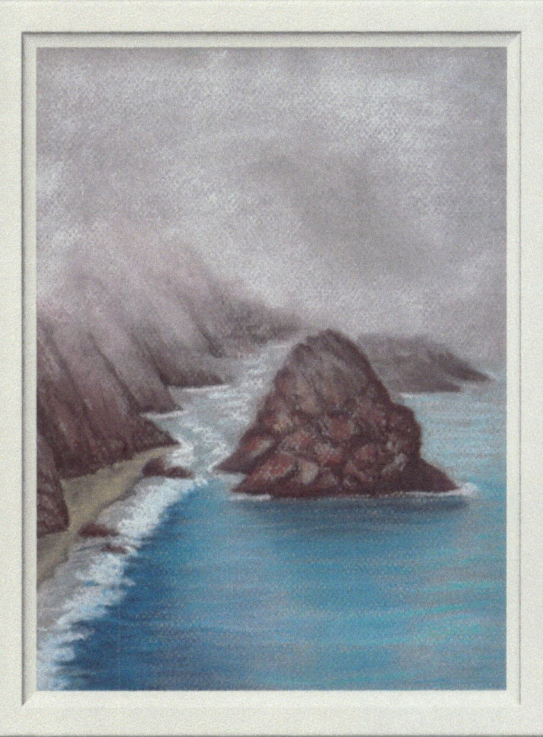

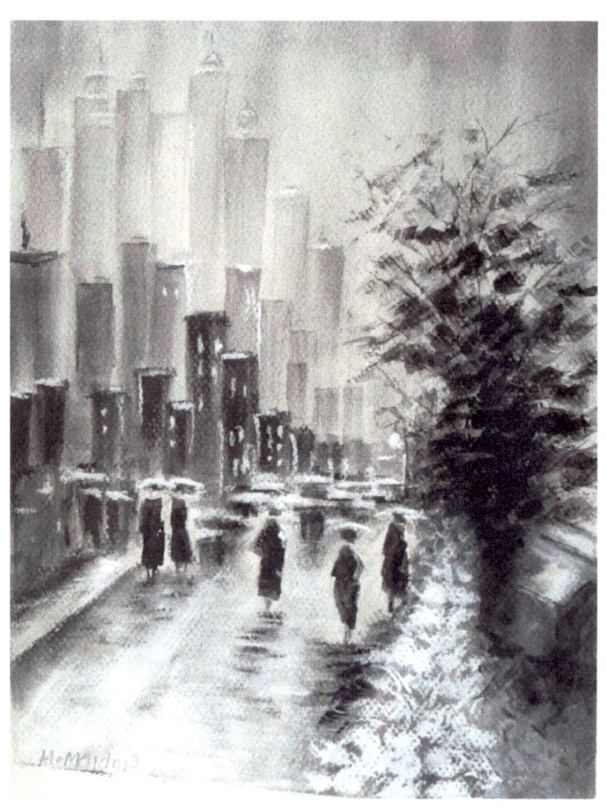

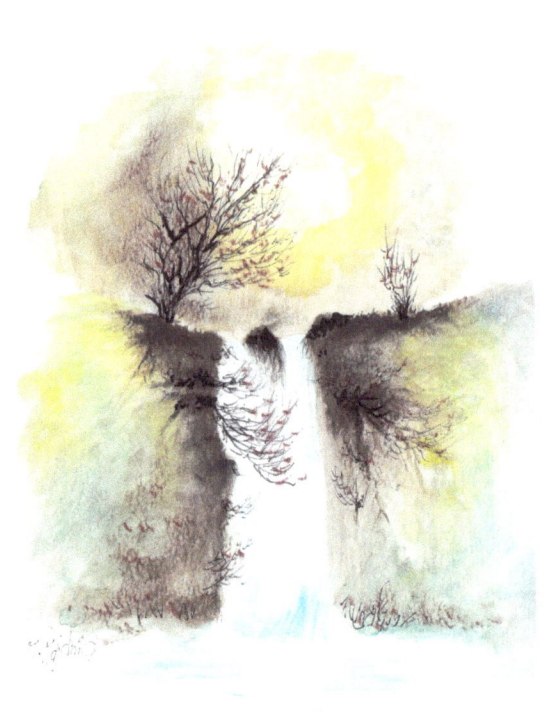

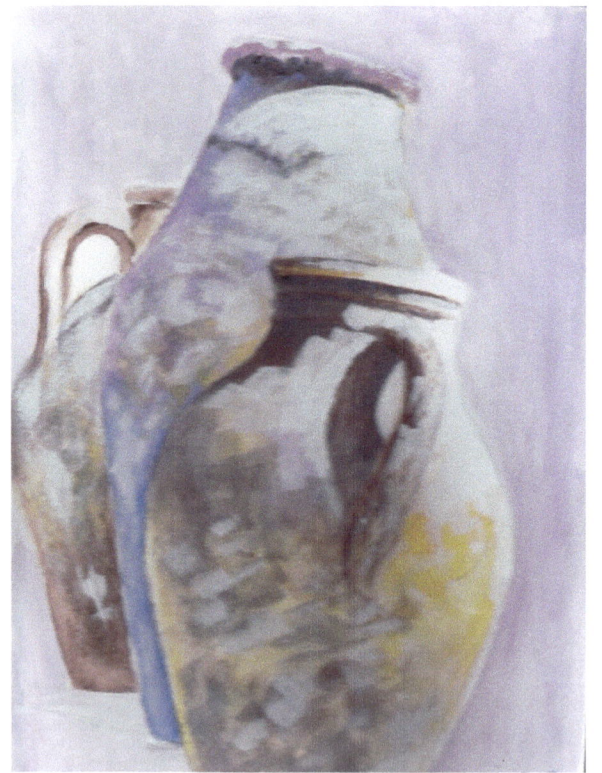

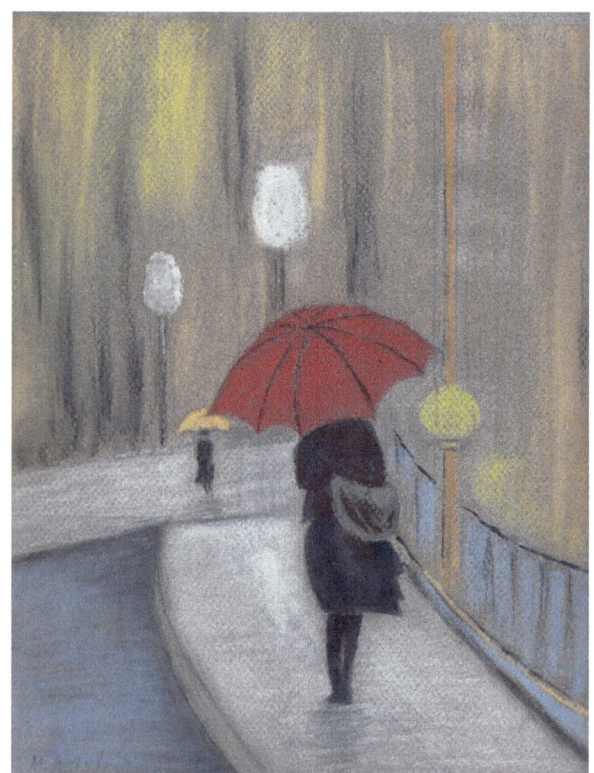

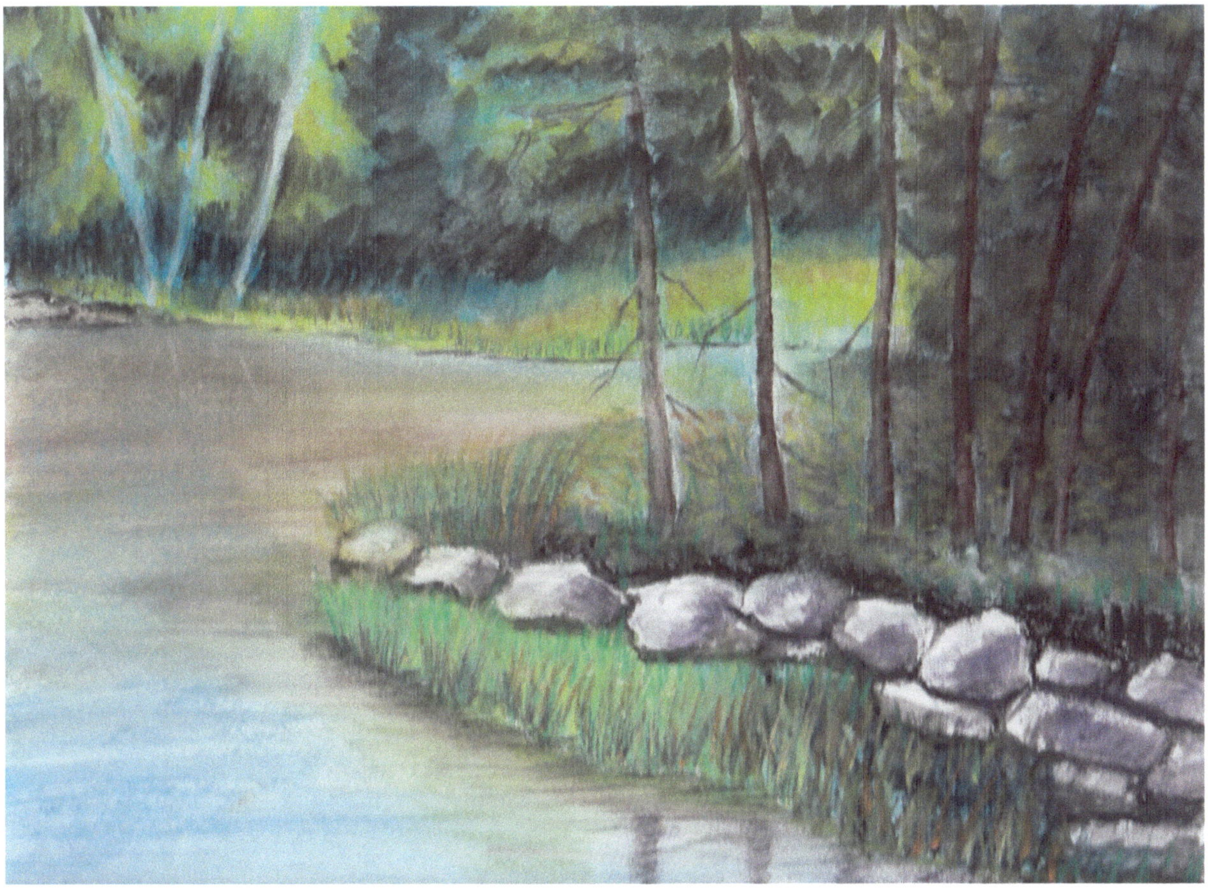

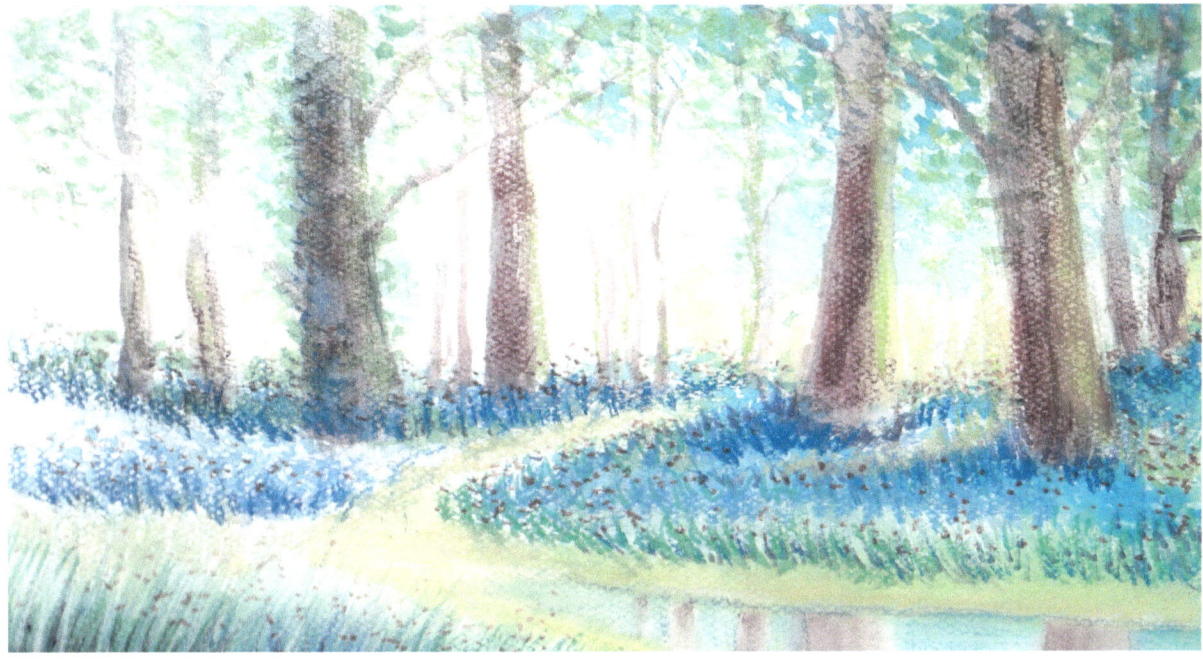

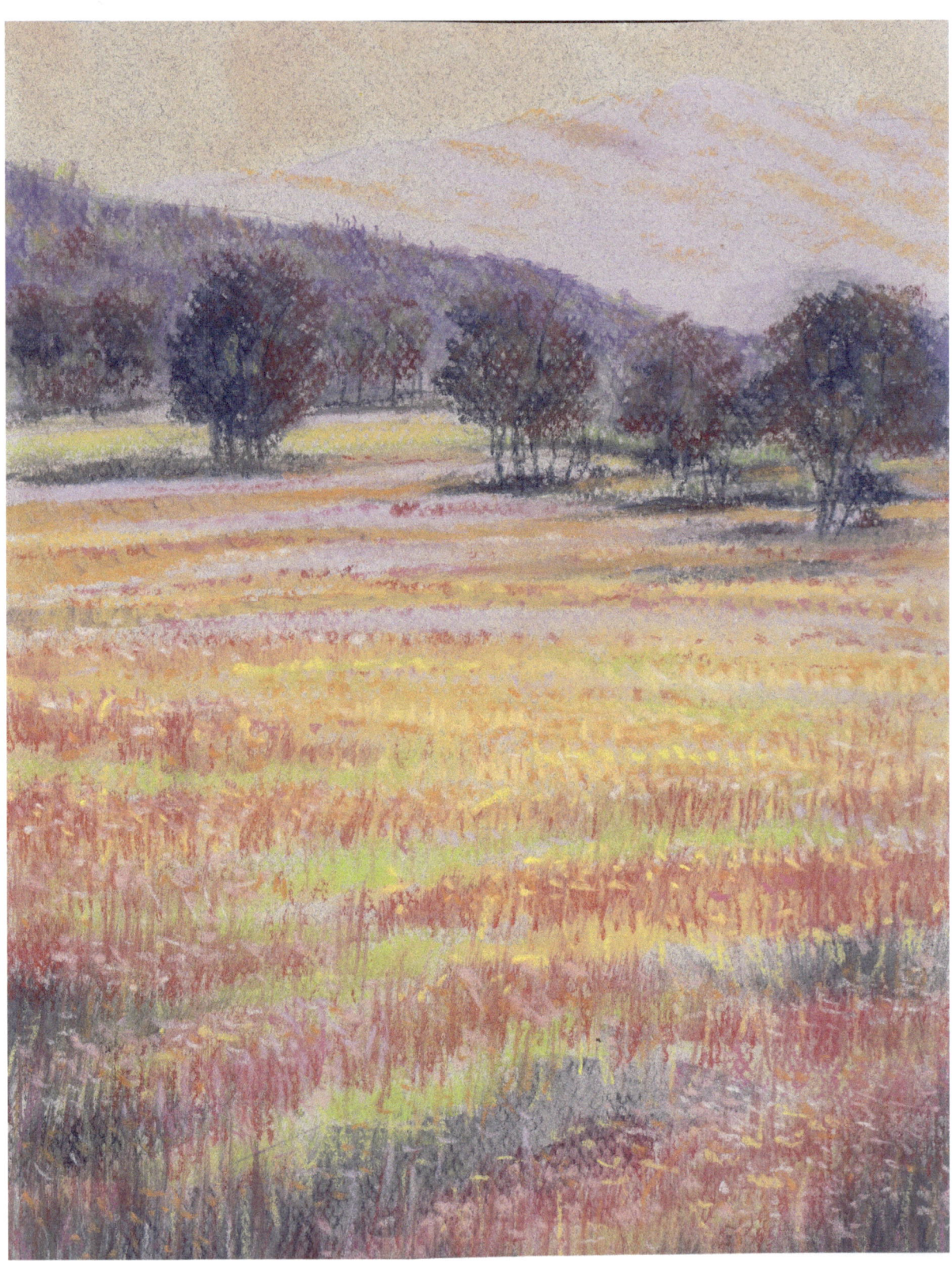

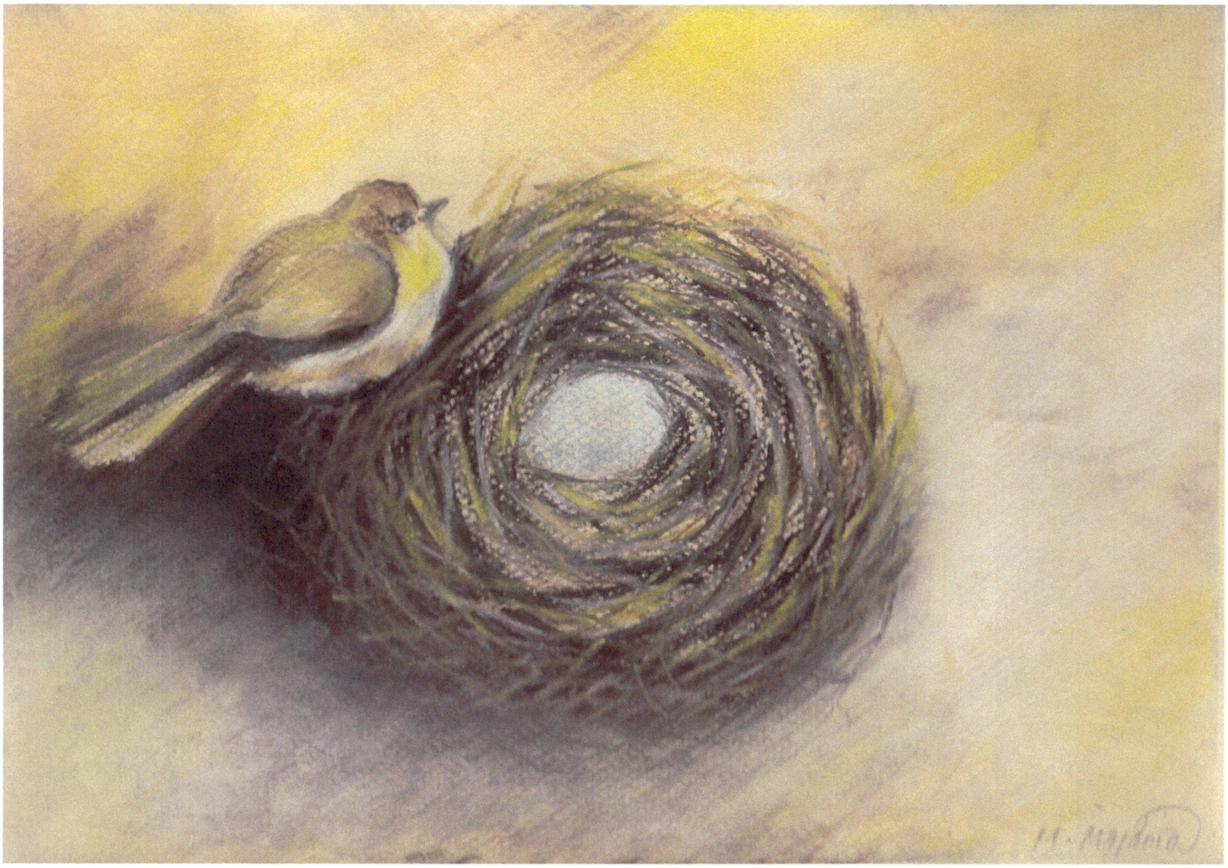

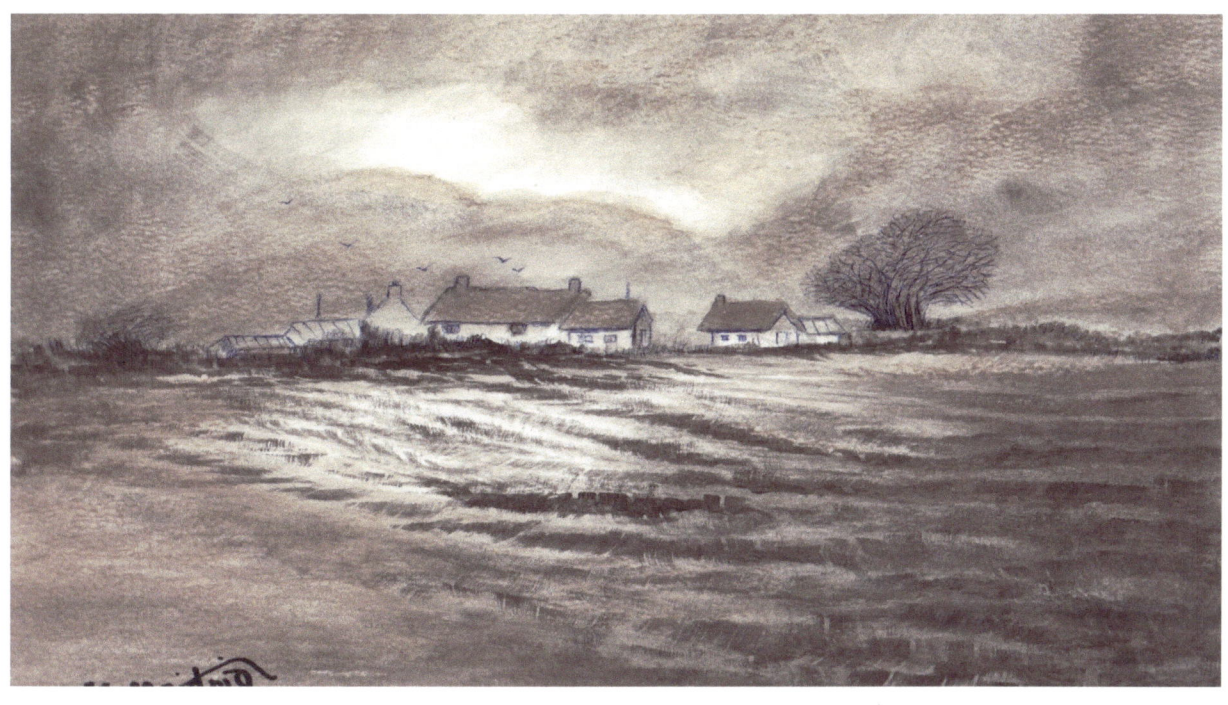

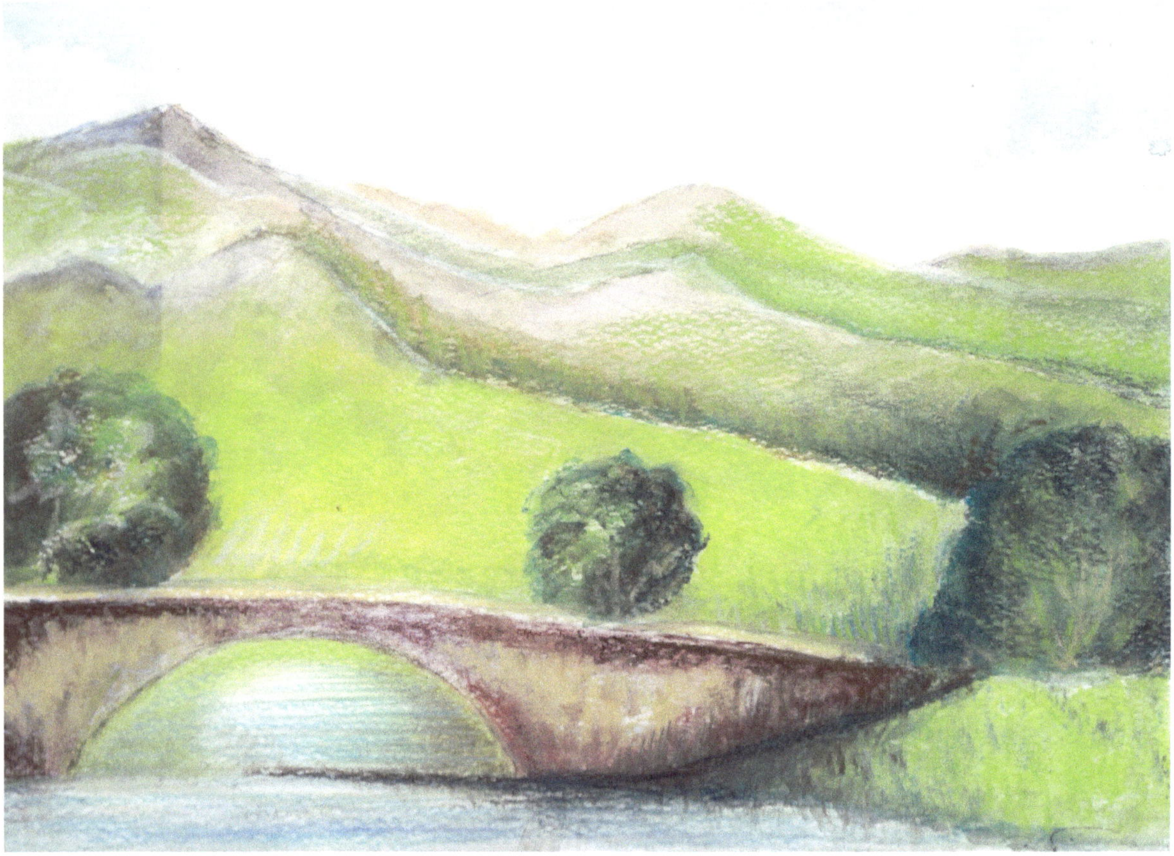

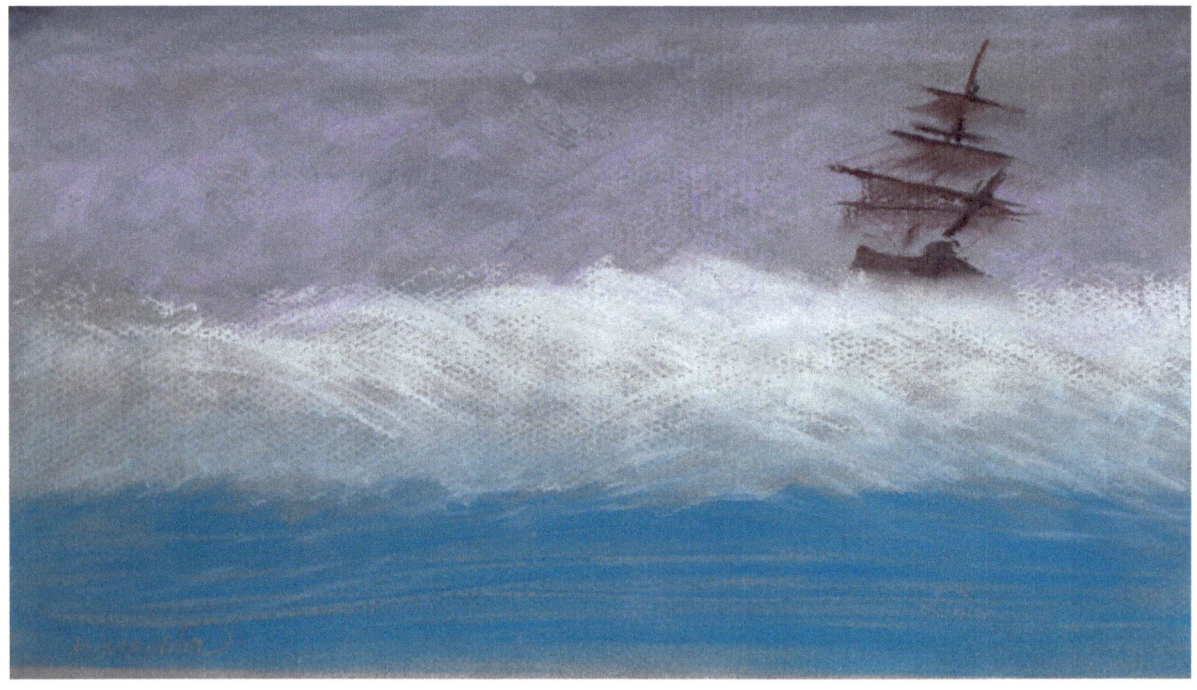

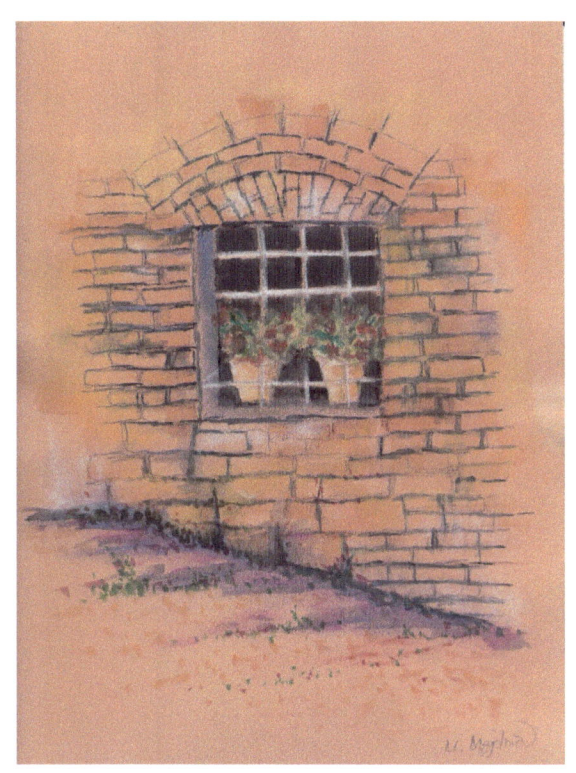

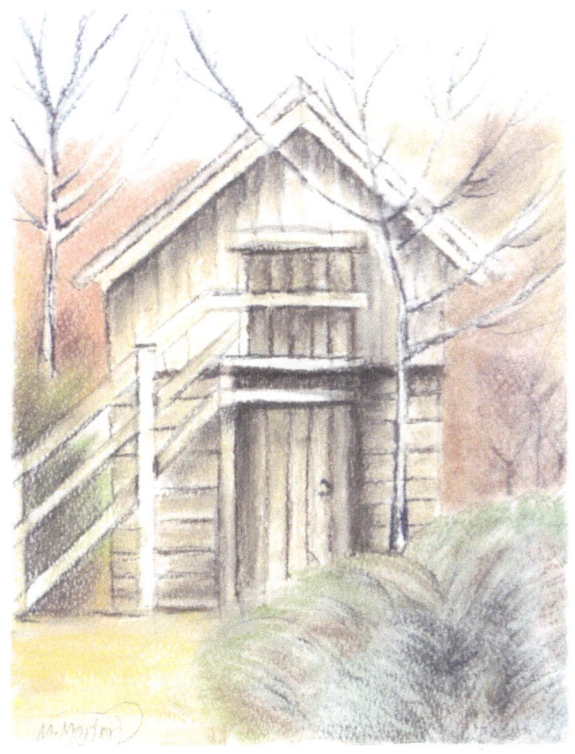

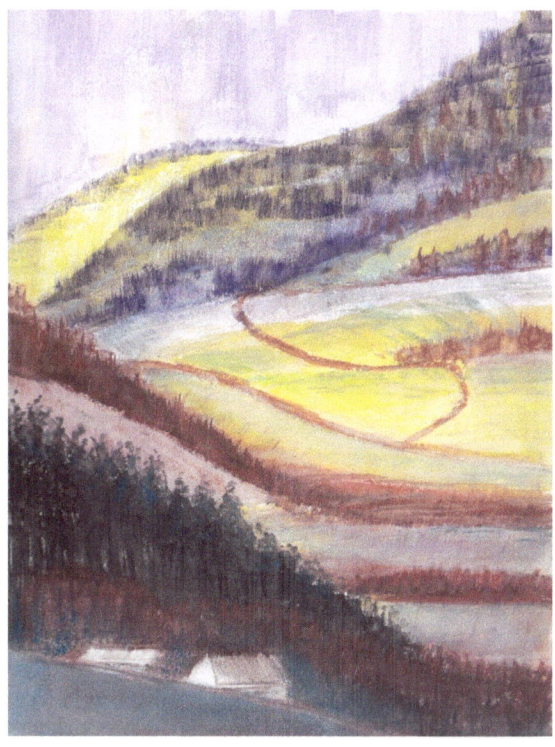

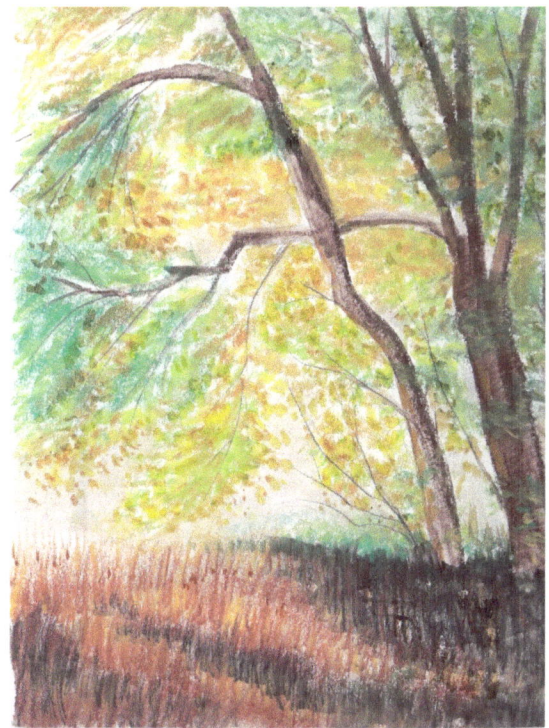

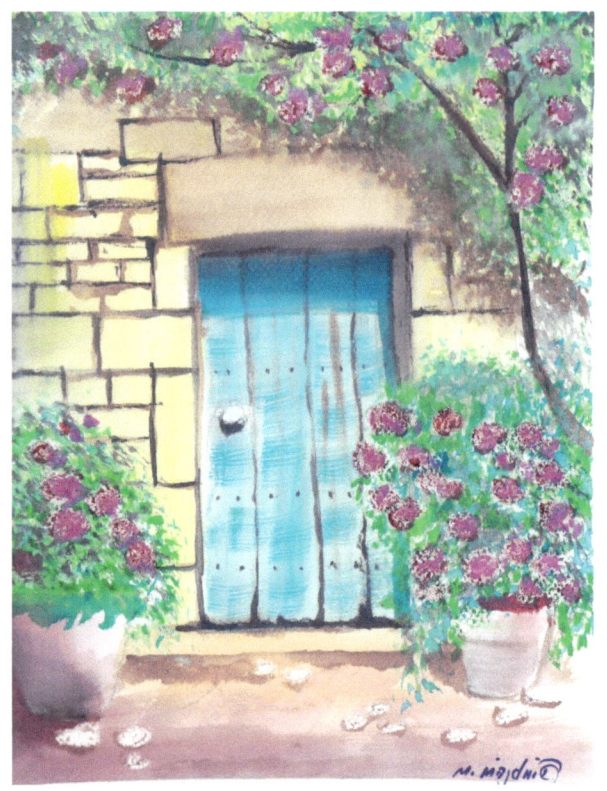
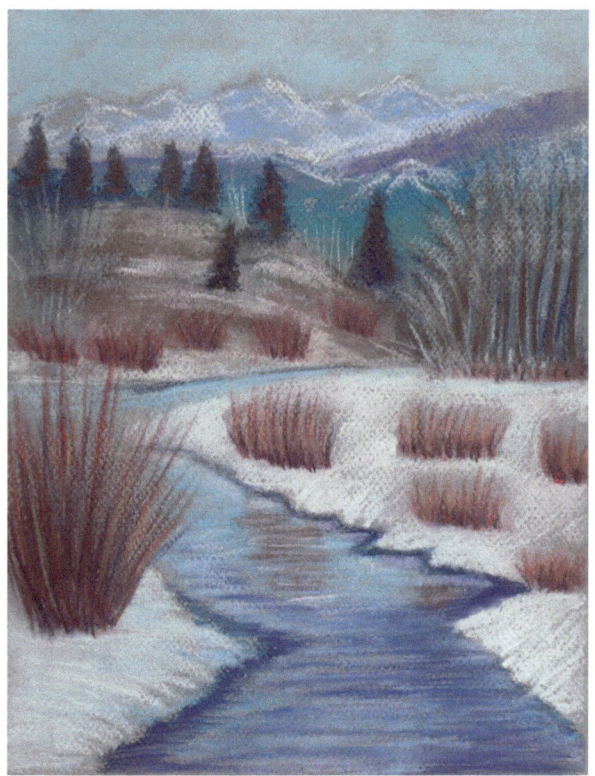
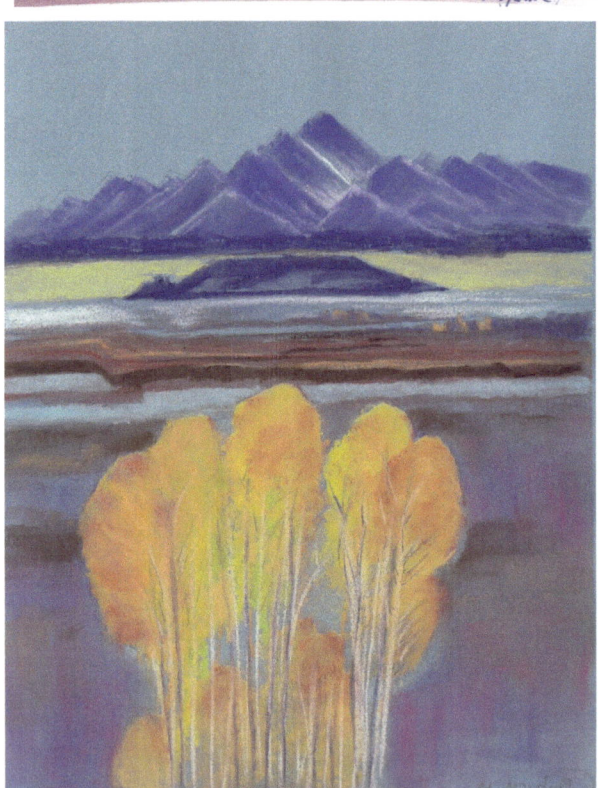
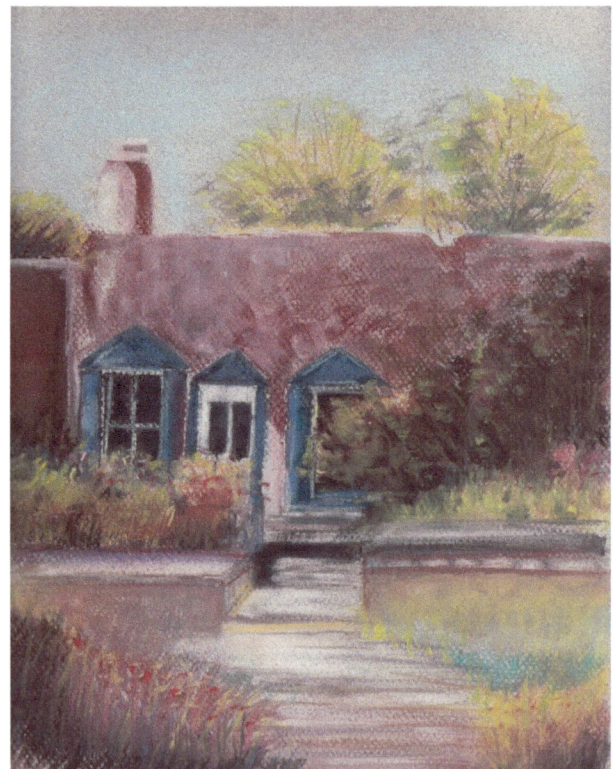

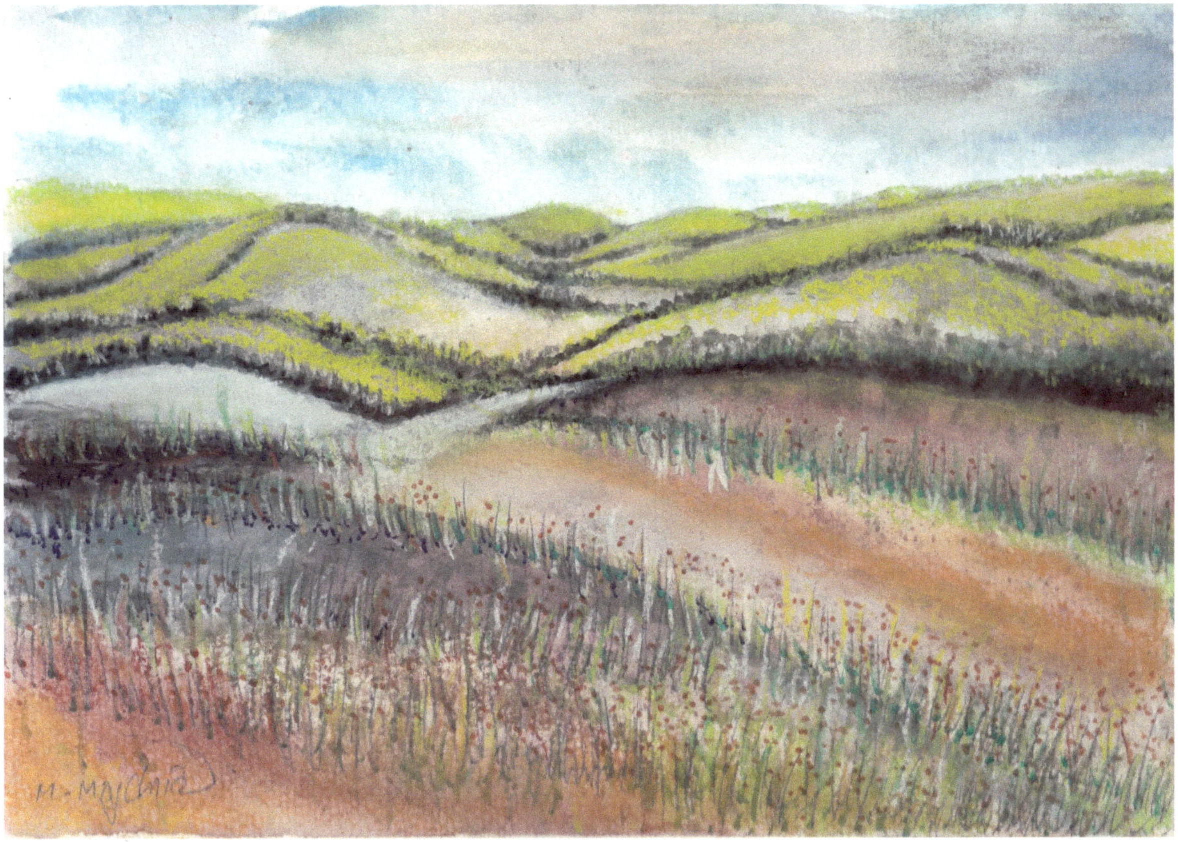

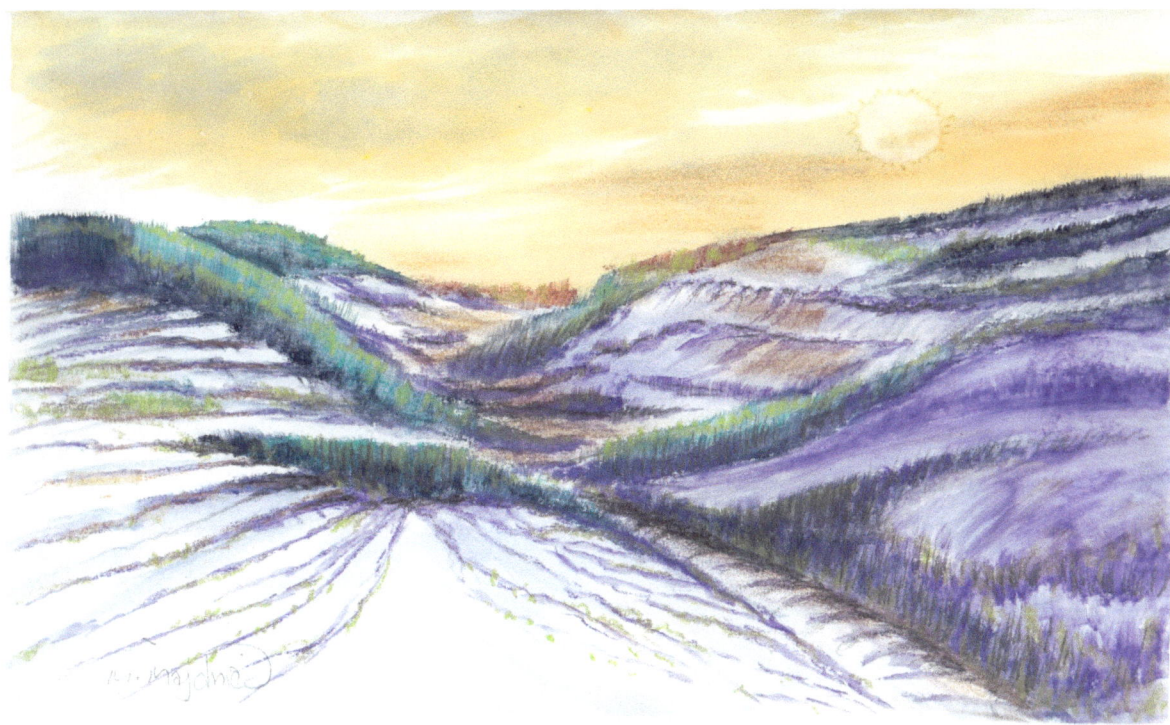

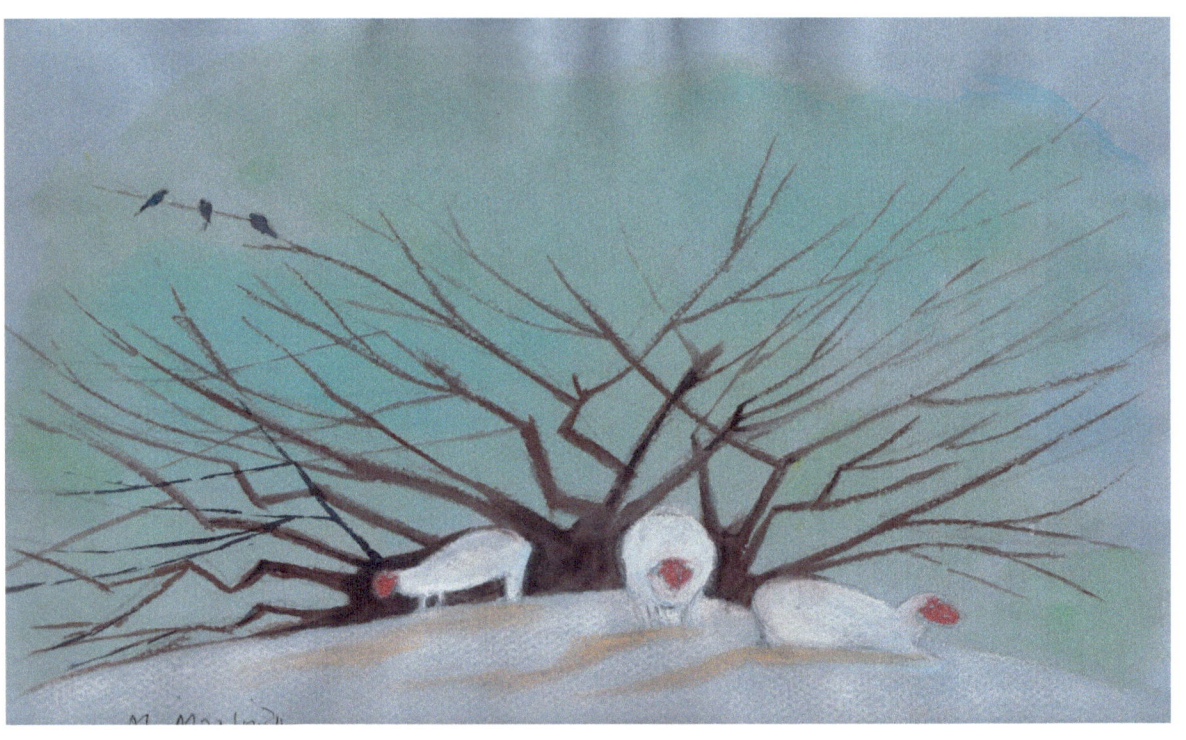

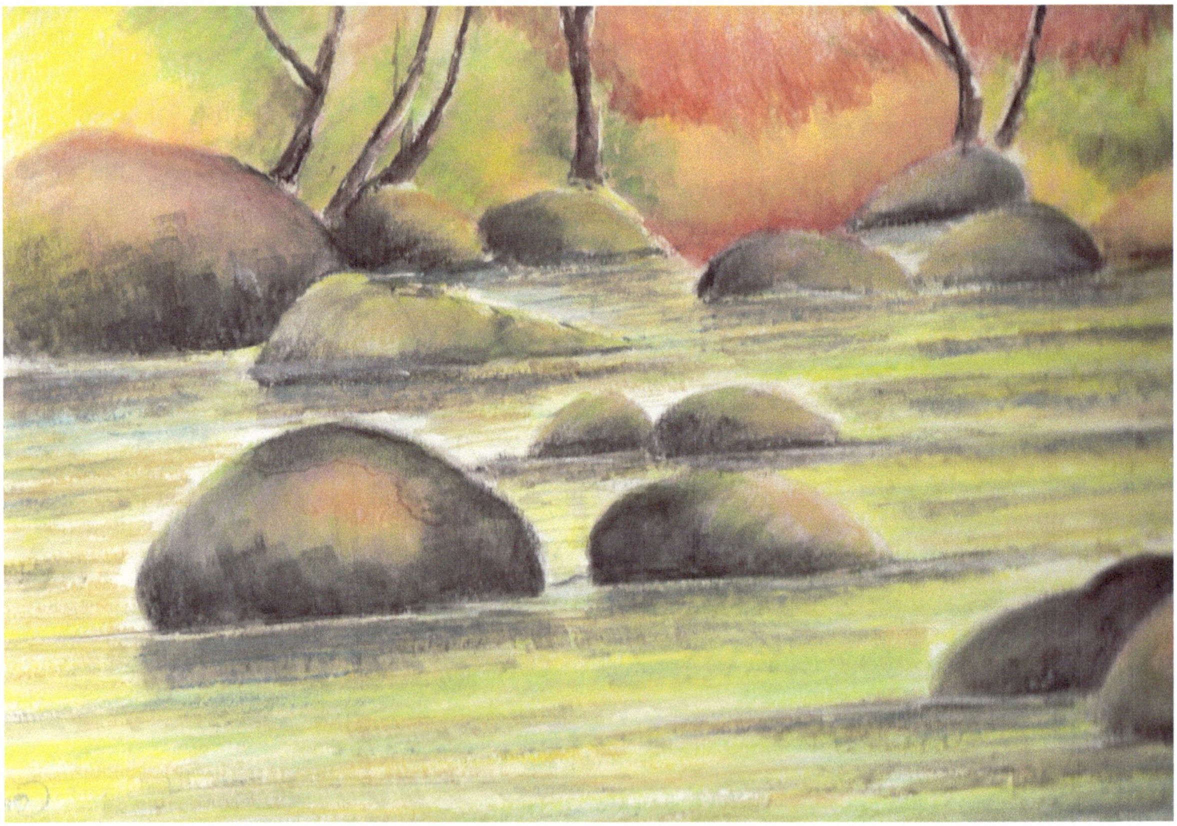

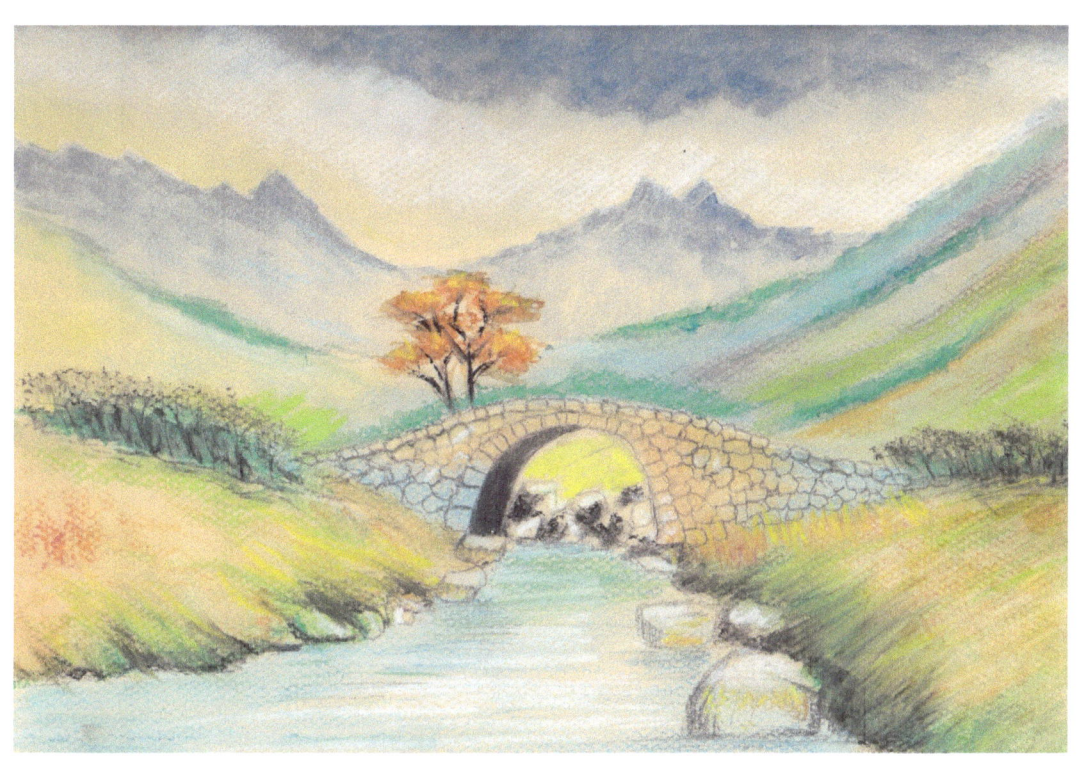

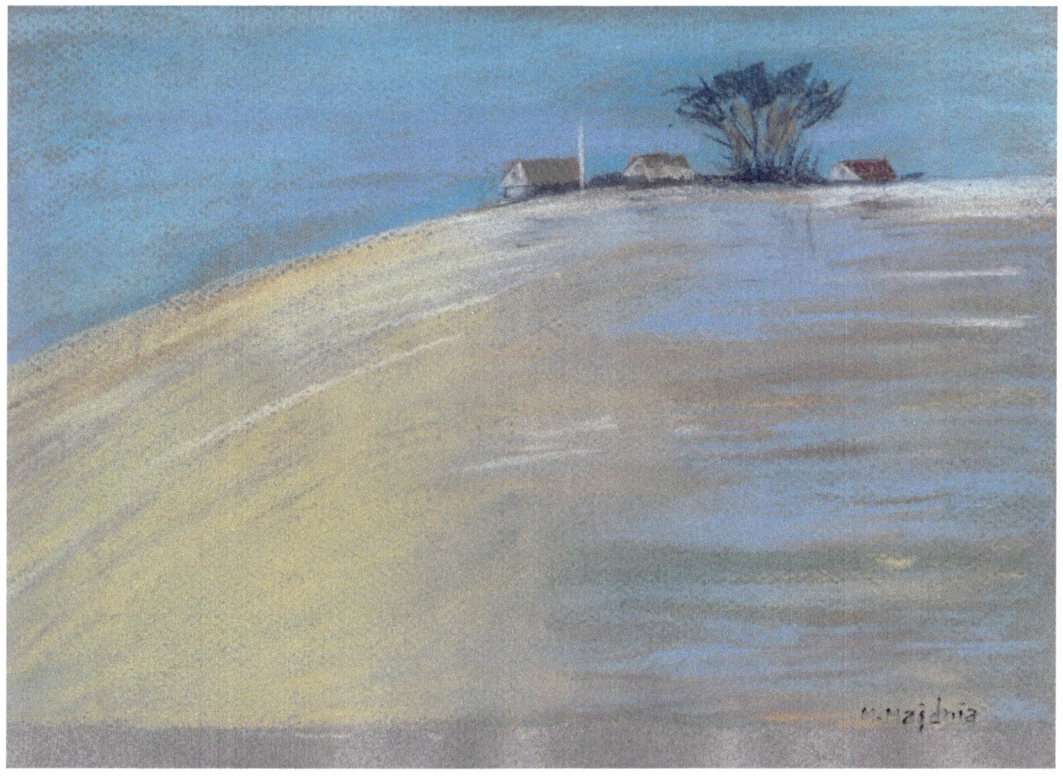

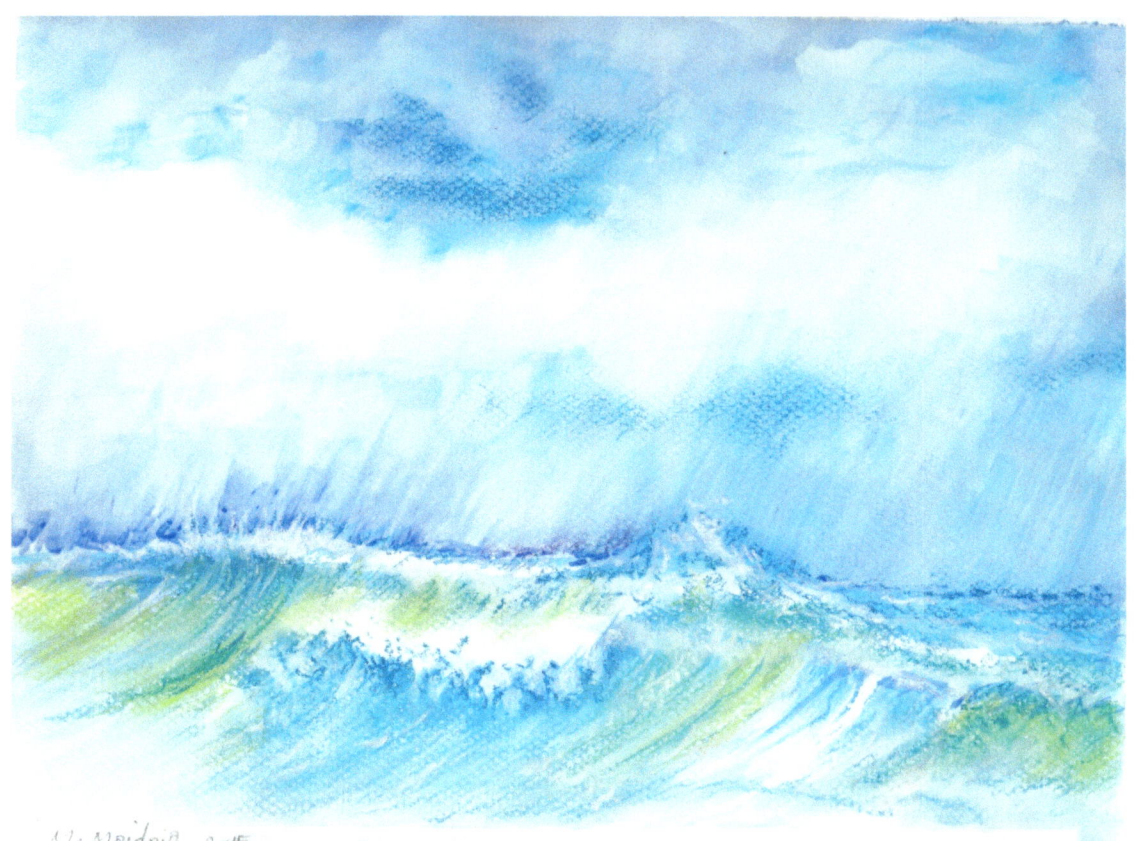

M. Majidnia 2015

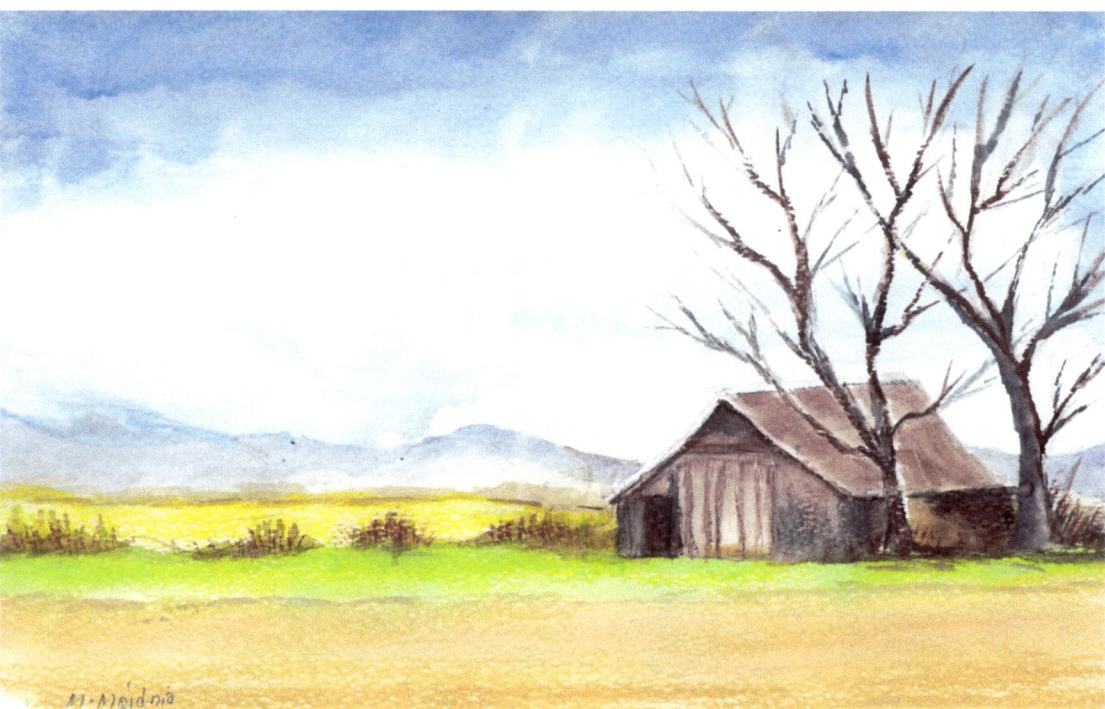

M. Majidnia

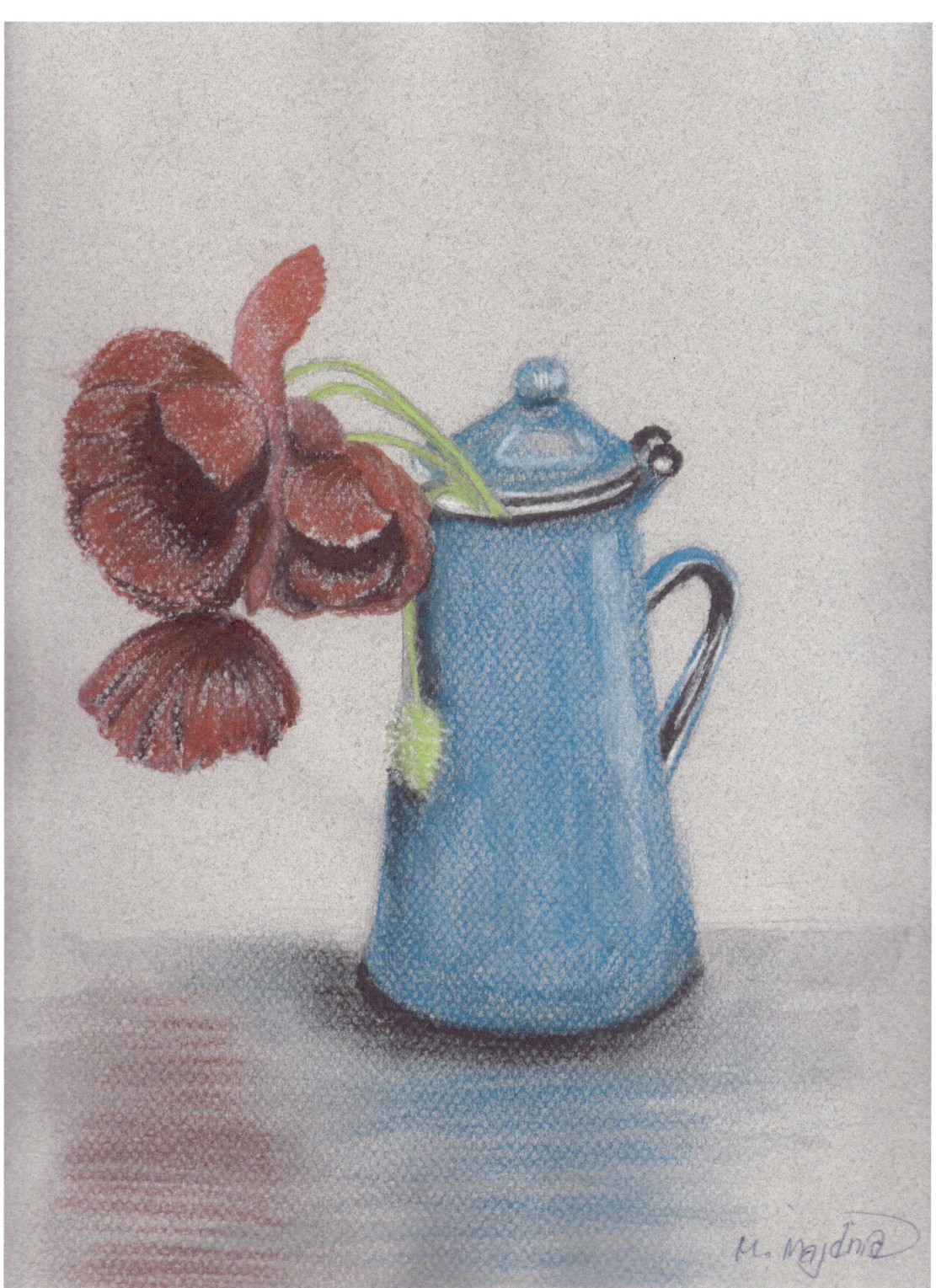

M. Majdina

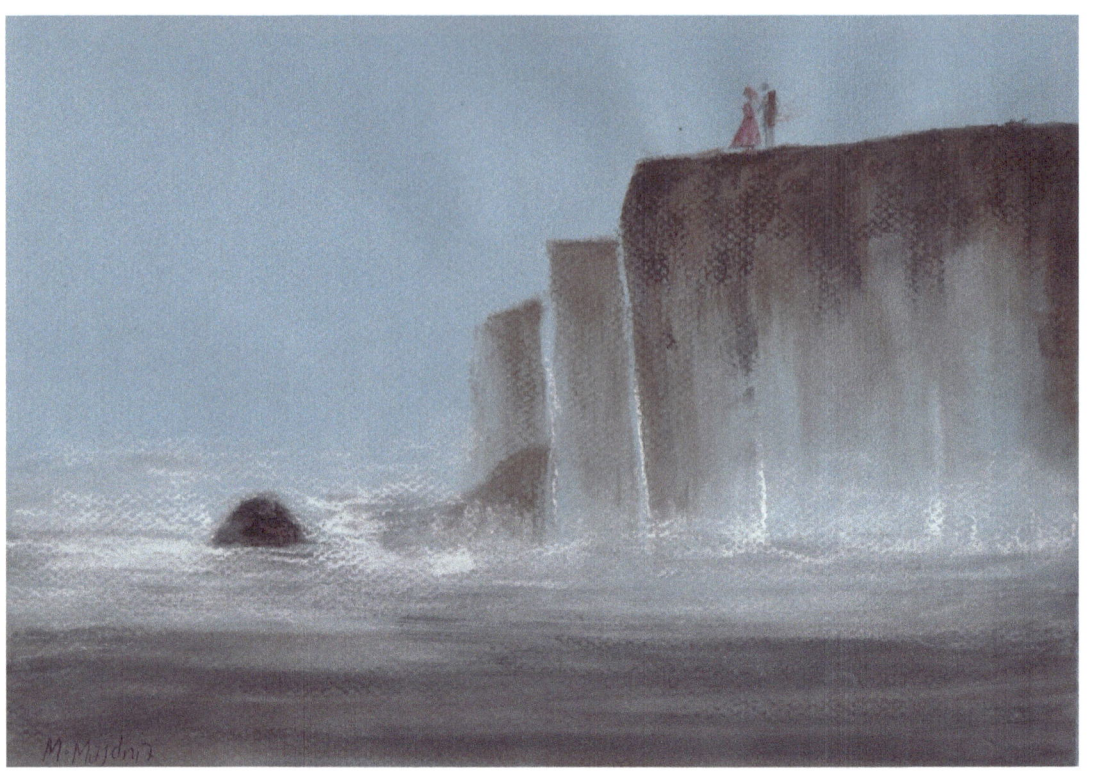

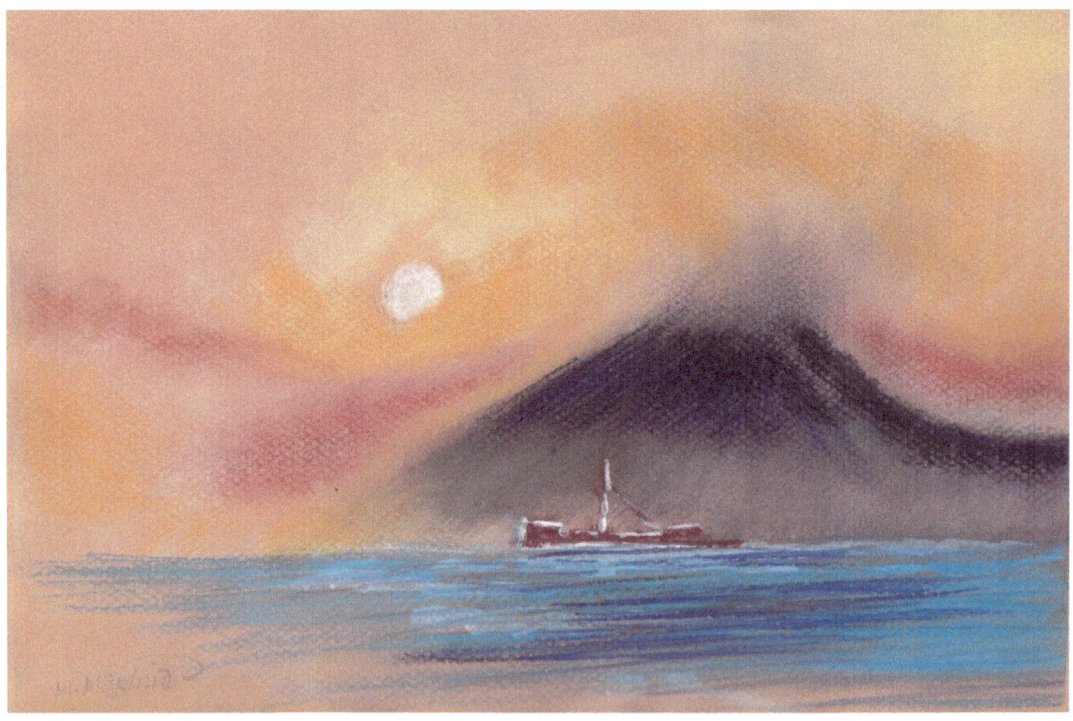

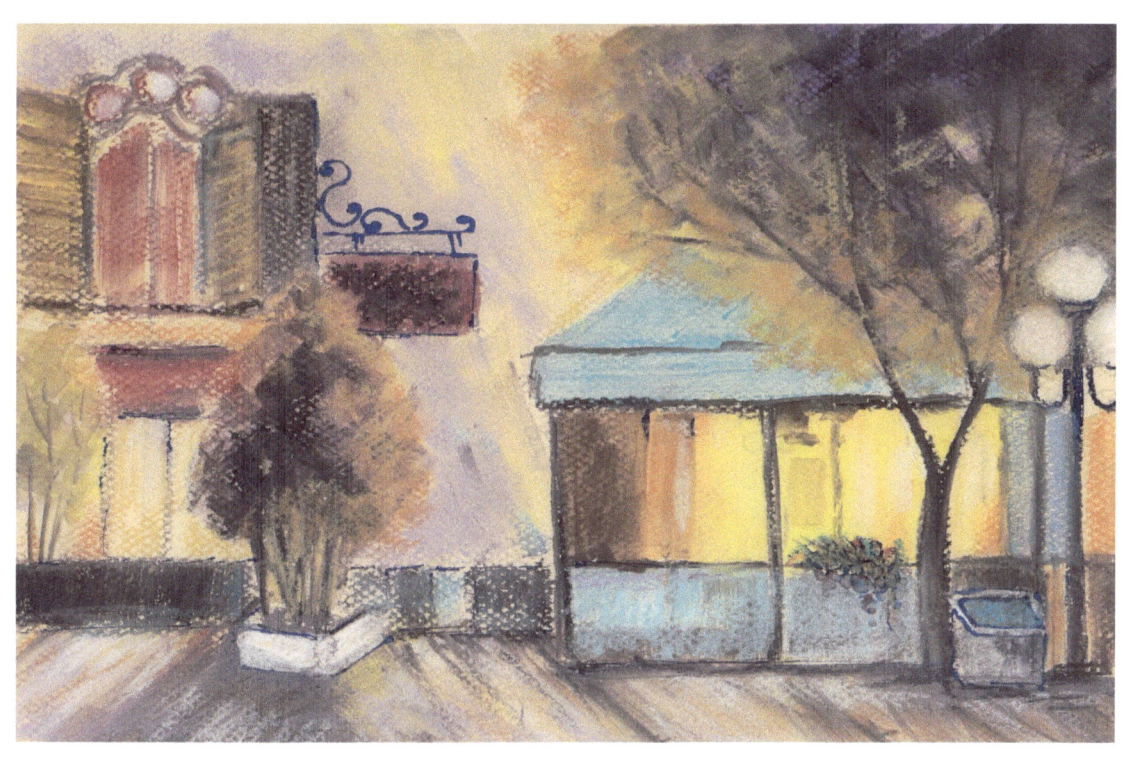

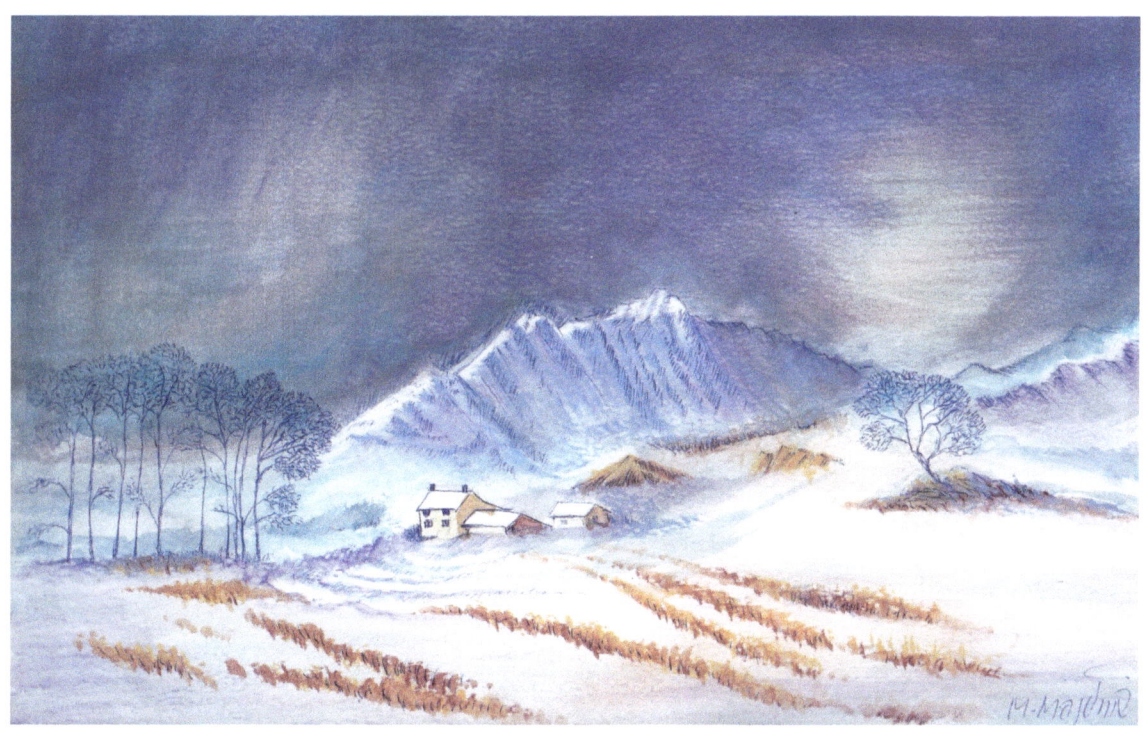

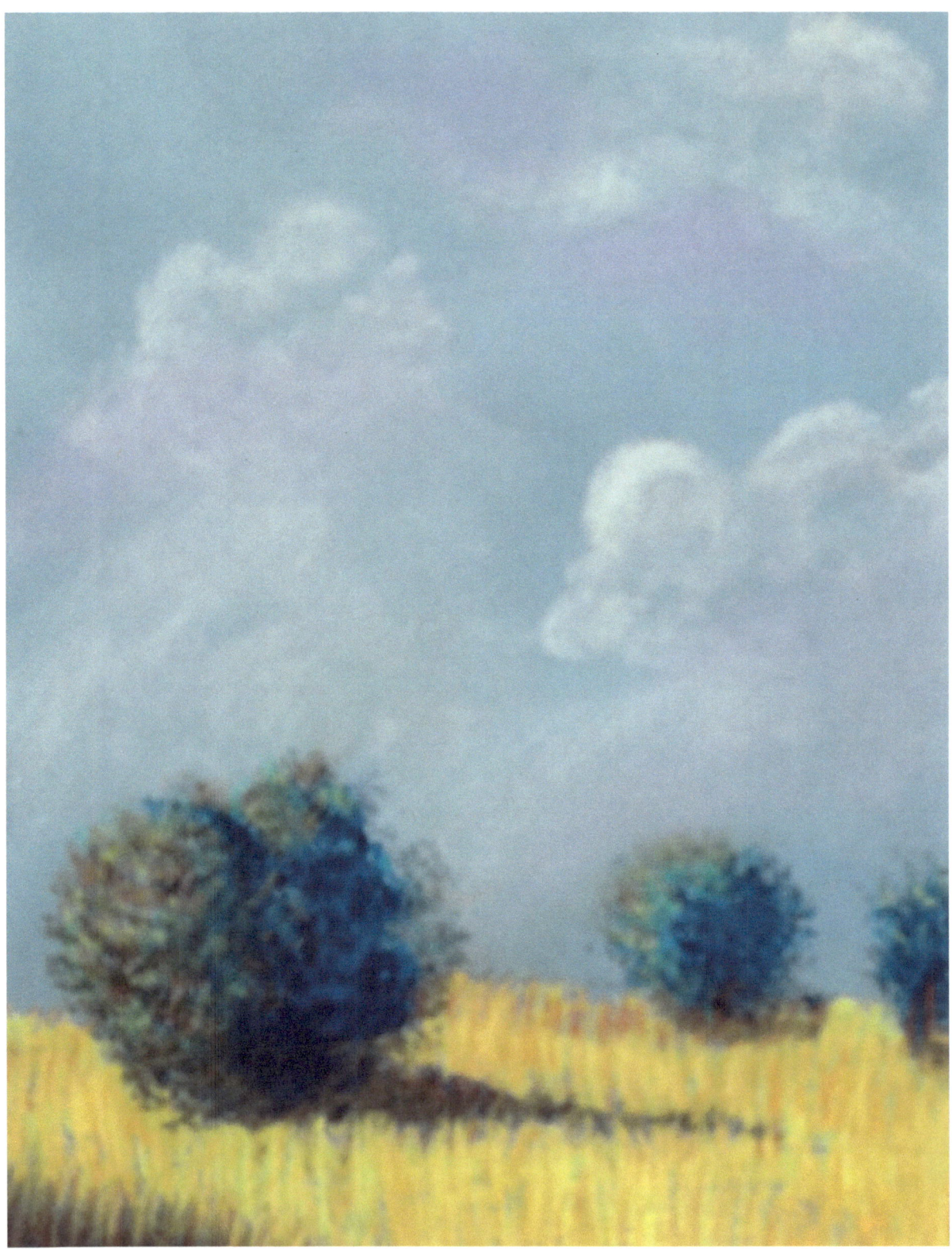

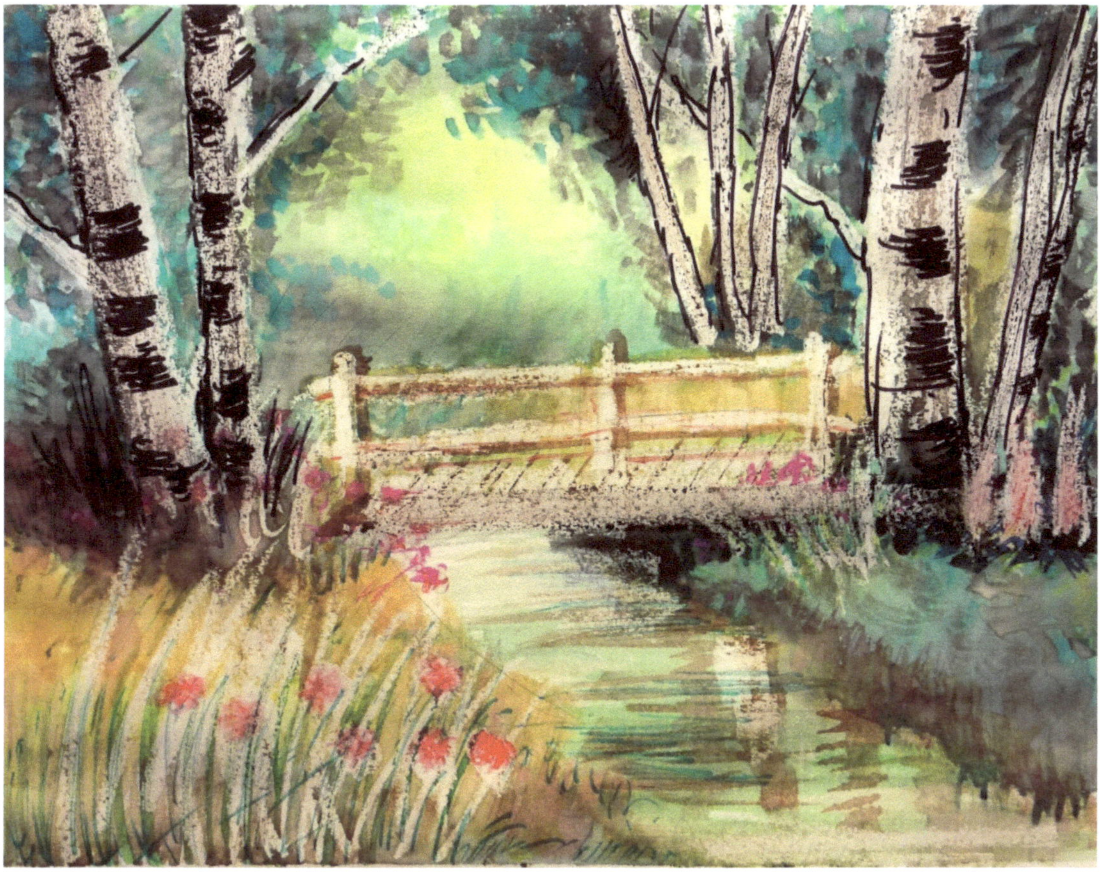

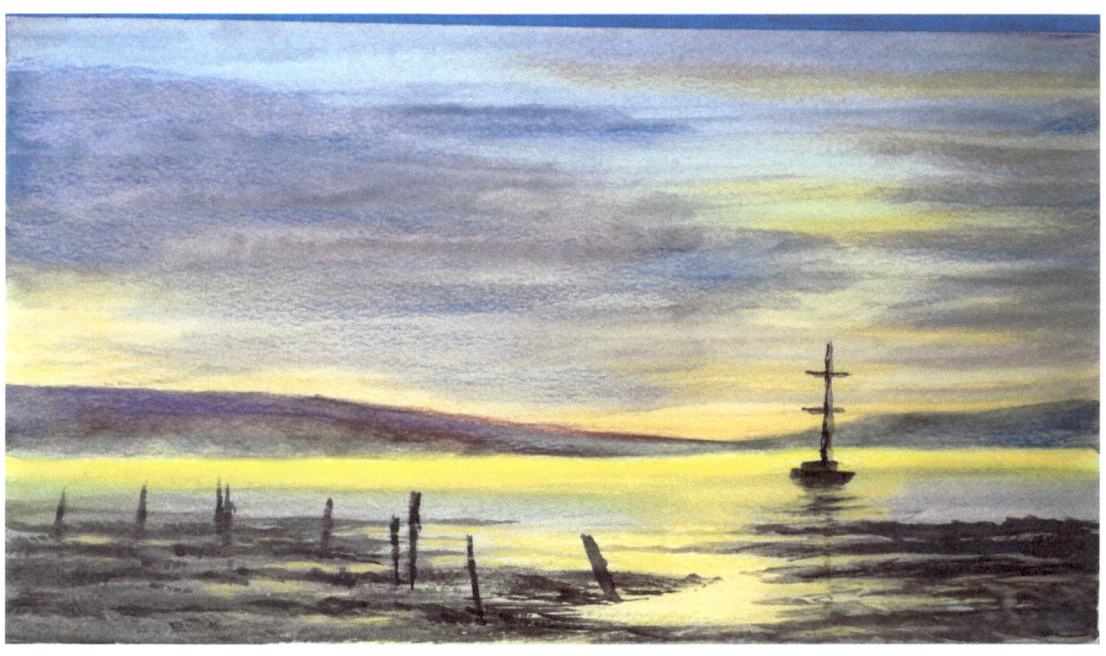

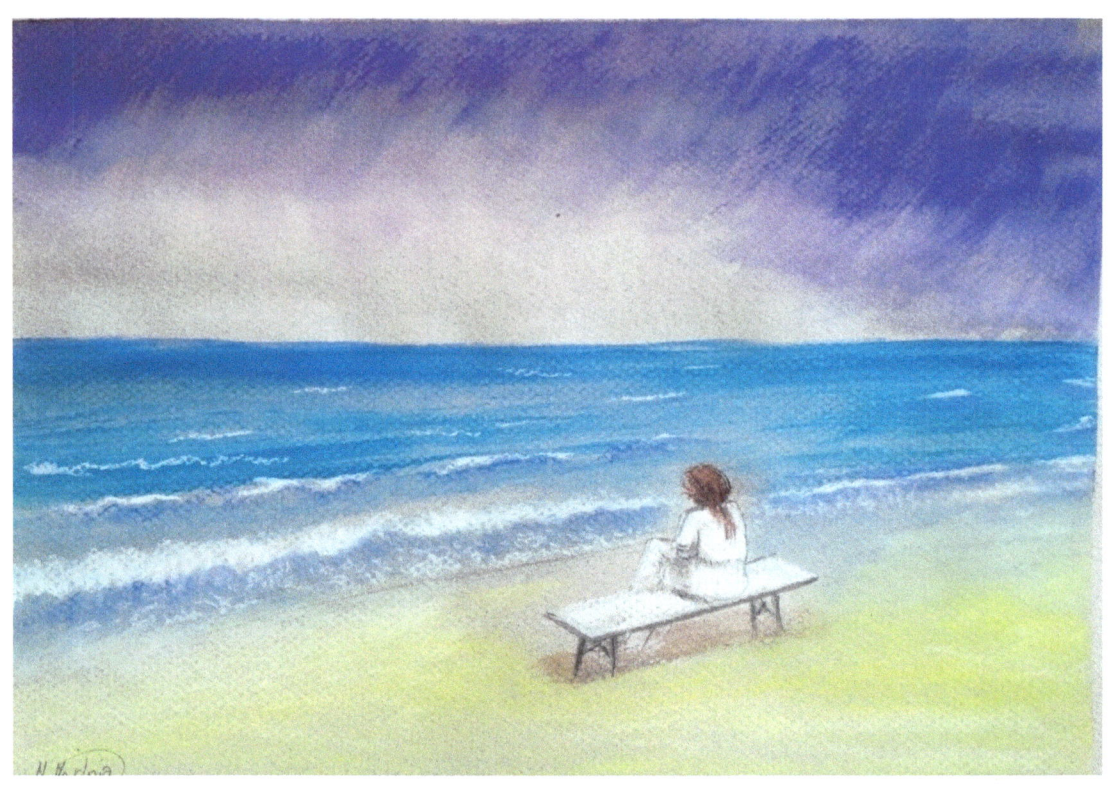

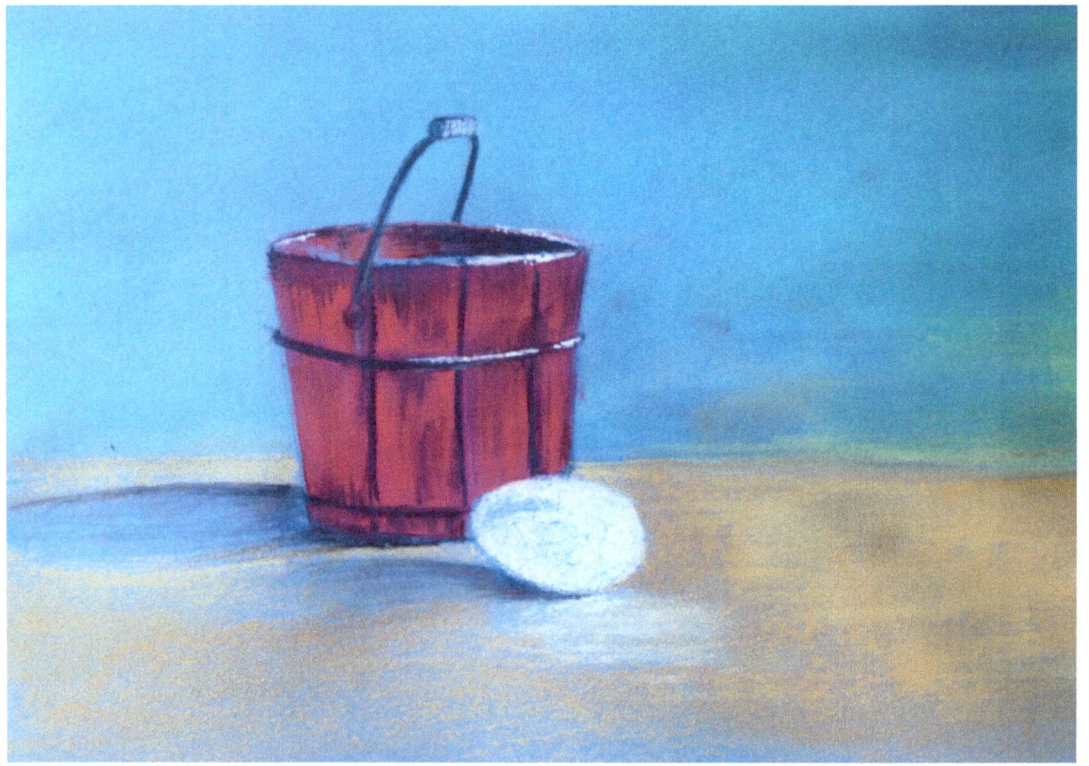

www.ingramcontent.com/pod-product-compliance
Lightning Source LLC
Chambersburg PA
CBHW050428180526
45159CB00005B/2451